DECISION
Mark Link, S.J.

**A meditation program
based on
*The Spiritual Exercises of St. Ignatius***

D1362061

Valencia, California   Allen, Texas

Imprimi Potest
Robert A. Wild, S.J.

Nihil Obstat
Msgr. Joseph Pollard, S.T.D., V.F.
Censor Deputatus

Imprimatur
Most Rev. Roger M. Mahony, D.D.
Archbishop of Los Angeles

March 25, 1988

The *Nihil Obstat* and *Imprimatur* are official declarations that the work contains nothing contrary to Faith and Morals. It is not implied thereby that those granting the *Nihil Obstat* and *Imprimatur* agree with the contents, statements, or opinions expressed.

Photo Credits

Front Cover: Clyde H. Smith/Peter Arnold, Inc.
Black-and-white photography: Mark Link, S.J.

Send all inquiries to:
Tabor Publishing
25115 Avenue Stanford, Suite 130
Valencia, California 91355

Printed in the United States of America

ISBN 0-89505-654-2 (*Challange*)
ISBN 0-89505-655-0 (*Decision*)
ISBN 0-89505-656-9 (*Journey*)

2 3 4 5   91 90 89

CONTENTS

Physical exercises—swimming, climbing, hiking—are ways to improve circulation, breathing, and muscle tone. In short, they are ways to improve physical fitness and bodily health.

"Spiritual exercises"—meditation, contemplation, vocal prayer—are ways to do the same for the human spirit. In short, they are ways to improve spiritual fitness and spiritual health. The "spiritual exercises," or meditations, in this book have to do with spiritual fitness and spiritual health.

Decision is the second phase of a three-phase meditation program called The Challenge Program. The first phase is found in a companion book called *Challenge;* the third phase, in a final book called *Journey.* The Challenge Program is based on *The Spiritual Exercises of St. Ignatius.* For a brief description of Saint Ignatius' Exercises, see Appendix A in the back of this book.

There are three ways you can use *Decision.* An ideal way is with the help of a spiritual guide and as part of a support group (eight to ten people) that meets weekly with the guide. The guide's role is discussed in Appendix B. The format for the group meetings is discussed in Appendix C.

A second way to use *Decision* is alone, under the direction of a spiritual guide.

A final way is by yourself, without a guide or a support group. This is not the best way, but it may be the only way possible for you. If you follow this option, try to consult occasionally with a spiritual guide.

Lent 1988   Mark Link, S.J.

1
CALL OF THE LEADER

Why do certain people excite you?

*"Look,
the whole world has gone after him."* John 12:19

Crowds lined the streets of Springfield, Illinois. They cheered as President-elect Lincoln passed by on his way to the railway station. At the station, Lincoln mounted the steps of the train's observation platform. When the crowd stopped cheering, he said:

I now leave you. . . . Without the assistance [that comes from God] I cannot succeed. With that assistance I cannot fail. . . . To his care commending you, as I hope in your prayers you will commend me, I bid you an affectionate farewell.

Abraham Lincoln was a man people could trust. He was a leader they could follow.

This first set of meditations focuses on great leaders and what gives them the power to inspire other people. The grace you seek in each exercise is the same:

Lord, let the example of great leaders
inspire me to do great things.

1

As you begin the second phase of this meditation program, it may be well to review the procedure for meditating on each exercise. It involves three steps:

1. *Preparation*—setting the stage for meditation
2. *Presence*—creating the climate for meditation
3. *Prayer*—meditating

Begin step one by recalling the grace you seek through your meditation. This grace differs each week and is specified in the introduction to the week.

Next, read the Scripture passage that gives the theme of the daily meditation. After reading it, pause briefly to review it in your mind and to let it sink into your heart.

Next, read the story that develops the theme of the daily meditation. Again, pause briefly to review it in your mind and to let it sink into your heart.

Lastly, *reread* the Scripture passage slowly and prayerfully. It is God's Word.

Step two consists in putting yourself in God's presence. One way to do this is to close your eyes, relax your body, and monitor your breathing.

As you focus on your breathing, recall that breath points to God's presence within you. The Book of Genesis says, "The LORD God . . . formed a man . . . he breathed life-giving breath into his nostrils and the man began to live."   *Genesis 2:7 (TEV)*

Once you have placed yourself in God's presence, move on to step three. To facilitate your reflection on the Scripture passage and the meditation story, a brief meditation guide has been placed at the end of each story. The purpose of this guide is not to restrict your meditation, but to stimulate it. Use the guide or not, as you see fit.

Conclude your meditation by doing two things: (1) reread the Scripture passage prayerfully, and (2) speak to God from your heart, as the Spirit moves you.

Day one

*You must shine among them like stars
lighting up the sky,
as you offer them the message of life.*
Philippians 2:15–16 (TEV)

One night Jay Kesler was walking through the slums of Calcutta. Suddenly he heard a strange sound. He turned around and saw a crippled boy hobbling toward him, begging for money. Jay gave the youngster a handful of coins. Seconds later Jay heard a terrible commotion. He turned around again. This time he saw the crippled child being beaten and robbed by a gang of older beggars.

A woman came into this same area one day and decided something had to be done. She spent everything she had on an old building, turning it into a school for small children. She had no desks, no chairs, no table. Her chalkboard was the building's dirt floor, which she rubbed smooth with an old rag and wrote on with a stick.

In the years that followed, the woman's dedication to the poor of Calcutta inspired others to join her. Today Mother Teresa has 80 fully equipped schools, 300 modern mobile dispensaries, 70 leprosy clinics, 30 homes for the dying, 30 homes for abandoned children, and 40,000 volunteers helping her worldwide.

How does Mother Teresa differ from most other leaders today? What makes people want to follow her? *Speak to Jesus about the need for leaders like Mother Teresa.*

Day two

The LORD said, "There—anoint him. . . ."
Then . . . the spirit of the LORD
rushed upon David.   1 Samuel 16:12-13

England's Duke of Wellington is reported to have said of Napoleon: "That man's presence on the battlefield is worth 40,000 soldiers."

The biblical King David possessed a similar kind of magical power that lifted the souls of his followers and drew from them a great loyalty.

During one battle, David was severely pressed. Afterward he was utterly exhausted and remarked that he would give anything for a drink of water from his favorite well, which lay on the other side of the enemy lines, several miles away.

Without hesitation three of his men stole through the enemy lines, drew water from the well, and brought it back to David. The king was deeply moved but refused to drink it. Instead he poured it out as an offering to the Lord and said, "God forbid that I should do such a thing! Could I drink the blood of these men who risked their lives?"   *1 Chronicles 11:19*

What one quality, above all others, do you look for in a leader? Why this one? *Speak to Jesus about the quality he looked for in those he chose to be leaders.*

Day three

Put away
the old self of your former way of life . . .
and put on the new self.   Ephesians 4:22, 24

The *Dallas Morning News* carried a story about swimmer Jeff Kostoff. Jeff's list of records and medals fills a page of Stanford's swimming guide. But missing from the list is mention of Jeff's best high school friend. Jeff says:

He was a swimmer, too, but he wasn't that talented. He realized the talent I had, and convinced me to stop screwing around and concentrate on swimming.

Jeff's comment recalls the words of Ralph Waldo Emerson: "Our chief want in life is someone who shall make us do what we can." Jeff's comment also recalls the words of Cardinal Duval, who wrote to his flock:

No matter how beautifully expressed, abstract ideas rarely move people. But let a person come forward, a living person, capable of speaking to the heart; let truth flow from the person's life, and let the person's power be matched by an equal gift of love; and the dawn of better days . . . will brighten our skies.

What does Cardinal Duval mean when he speaks of a person "capable of speaking to the heart"? Can you think of someone you know who speaks to your heart? *Speak to Jesus about his capability of speaking to the human heart.*

Day four

Jesus went around to all the towns. . . .
At the sight of the crowds,
his heart was moved with pity for them
because they were troubled and abandoned,
like sheep without a shepherd.   Matthew 9:35–36

The morale of the Northern army dipped to zero in September of 1862. A miracle was needed to reverse the situation. The person President Lincoln chose to work that miracle was General McClellan, who had trained many of the Northern troops.

McClellan mounted his black horse and cantered down the dusty roads of Virginia. He met the retreating troops, waved his cap, and shouted words of encouragement. When the beaten troops saw their old teacher, something ignited inside them. Here is how Bruce Catton, the great Civil War historian, describes the scene in *This Hallowed Ground:*

Down mile after mile of Virginia roads the stumbling columns came alive, and threw caps and knapsacks into the air, and yelled until they could yell no more . . . because they saw this dapper little rider outlined against the purple starlight. And this, in a way, was the turning point of the war. . . . No one could ever quite explain it.

Whatever it was, Lincoln got his miracle, and history was changed forever.

Recall a time when someone put you in a leadership role. What effect did the responsibility have on you? *Speak to Jesus about this.*

6

*Jesus, looking at him, loved him
and said to him, "You are lacking in one thing.
Go, sell what you have . . .
then come, follow me."* Mark 10:21

The *London Times* carried this tiny ad in the early 1900s. No picture accompanied it.

Wanted: Persons for dangerous journey. Small wages, bitter cold, long months of complete darkness, constant danger, safe return doubtful, honor and recognition if successful.—Sir Ernest Shackleton

Over five thousand people from all over England responded to that ad. From these applicants Shackleton chose twenty-eight to accompany him on an expedition to the South Pole.

The trip took place in 1915 aboard a ship called *Endurance.* In the course of the expedition, the *Endurance* got frozen into the ice "like an almond in a chocolate bar."

Eventually the ship was crushed by the ice, and the crew had to pull their supplies along on sleds. All, however, returned to honor and recognition. All agreed, also, that it was Shackleton's heroic leadership that spelled the difference between success and failure.

Are people today as open to a challenge as they once were? *Speak to Jesus about your own openness to a challenge, should the right person speak to your heart.*

Day six

*"If anyone wishes to come after me,
he must deny himself and take up his cross daily
and follow me."* Luke 9:23

Alan Paton has an inspiring conversation in his book *Oh, But Your Land Is Beautiful*. It's between a black person and a white person who have put their lives on the line for racial justice in South Africa. When the one remarks that they may end up with a lot of body scars, the other says:

Well, I look at it this way. When I get up there, the great Judge will say, "Where are your scars?" And if I haven't any, he will ask, "Were there no causes worthy of getting scars?"

That courageous remark recalls the words of President Theodore Roosevelt before an audience in Chicago:

Far better is it to dare mighty things, to win glorious triumphs, even though checkered by failures, than to rank with those poor spirits who neither enjoy much nor suffer much because they live in the gray twilight that knows neither victory nor defeat.

___

What is one of the most daring things you ever attempted? *Speak to Jesus about how Roosevelt's words apply to you.*

> *"Do not ask me to abandon . . . you!*
> *for wherever you go I will go,*
> *wherever you lodge I will lodge."*   Ruth 1:16

Imagine that a young, dynamic political leader emerges. It's clear—even to opponents—that this leader is not only gifted but also selfless and dedicated to serving others, especially the poor and the powerless.

More remarkably, this leader possesses a charism that cuts across every ethnic and social group. Everyone trusts this remarkable person. Everyone recognizes that the "hand of God" rests upon this leader.

Imagine an address the leader makes to the people. With remarkable compassion and understanding, the leader spells out programs for eradicating corruption, freeing cities of drug traffic and crime, renewing ghetto areas, reforming the prison system, erasing poverty.

Even the most realistic politicians are impressed by the leader's grasp of the problems and the insights for dealing with them. They conclude: "If it's possible to transform society, this young person is the one to do it."

The leader finishes addressing the people by asking for volunteers.

Would you volunteer? *Speak to Jesus about your willingness to sacrifice for such a leader and such a cause.*

2
CALL OF THE KING

How is Jesus different from other leaders?

"I am the way and the truth and the life." John 14:6

General Bertrand and Napoleon were talking about Jesus. Bertrand expressed the view that Jesus was not the Son of God, but simply a dynamic human leader, like Napoleon himself.

Napoleon disagreed, saying that Jesus was able to do what no human leader has ever been able to do. He was able to impart something of himself and his own power to his followers. Napoleon put it this way:

I know men, and I tell you Jesus Christ is not a man. . . . I have so inspired multitudes that they would die for me . . . the lightning of my eye, my voice, a word from me, then the sacred fire was kindled in their hearts. I do, indeed, possess the secret of this magical power that lifts the soul, but I could never impart it to anyone. None of my generals ever learned it from me; nor have I the means of perpetuating my name and love for me in the hearts of men.

The meditation exercises that follow focus on Jesus and how he differed from other dynamic leaders. The grace you ask for in each exercise in this:

Lord, show me how you differ
from every other dynamic leader.

During the week ahead, the Holy Spirit may put into your heart the desire to pick up the Gospels and read about Jesus. Mark's Gospel is a good one to read. Mark focuses less on what Jesus says and more on what he does. Commenting on this, Alexander Jones says:

This is not to say that Mark's Gospel is a song without words. Rather, it is to say that the absence of many words leaves us freer to enjoy the melody which is the person and action of Jesus.

Day one

*Christ himself . . . left you an example,
so that you would follow in his steps.*
1 Peter 2:21 (TEV)

There was once a handsome prince who had a crooked back. This defect kept him from being the kind of prince he was meant to be. One day the king had the best sculptor in his kingdom make a statue of the prince. It portrayed him, however, not with a crooked back but with a straight back. The king placed the statue in the prince's private garden. When the prince saw it, his heart beat faster. Months passed and the people began to say, "The prince's back doesn't seem as crooked as it was." When the prince heard this, his heart beat even faster. Now the prince began to spend hours studying the statue and meditating on it. Then one day a remarkable thing happened. The prince found himself standing as straight as the statue.

That story is a parable of you and me. We too were born to be a prince or a princess. But a defect kept us from being the kind of person we were meant to be. Then one day God the Father sent his only Son, Jesus, into the world to show us what we were meant to be. Jesus stands spiritually straight, and when we look at him, our hearts beat faster.

What is there about Jesus that makes your heart beat faster? *Speak to Jesus about what there is in him that brings out the best in you.*

13

Day two

*To Jesus Christ be glory and power
forever and ever.* Revelation 1:6

Here is a young man who was born in an obscure village, the child of a peasant woman. . . . He worked in a carpenter shop until he was thirty. . . . He never wrote a book. He never held an office. He never owned a home. He never had a family. He never went to college. . . . He never did one of the things that usually accompany greatness. He had no credentials but himself.

While he was still a young man the tide of public opinion turned against him. His friends ran away. He was turned over to his enemies. . . . He was nailed to a cross between two thieves. While he was dying, his executioners gambled for the only piece of property he had on earth, and that was his coat. When he was dead, he was laid in a borrowed grave through the pity of a friend.

Nineteen centuries have come and gone, and today he is . . . the leader of the column of progress. I am far within the mark when I say that all the armies that ever marched, and all the kings who ever reigned, put together, have not affected the life of man upon this earth as has that One Solitary Life. Anonymous

Reread this piece slowly. *Pause after reading each paragraph to speak to Jesus and to listen to him speak to your heart.*

Day three

*"I am the light of the world.
Whoever follows me will not walk in darkness,
but will have the light of life."*   John 8:12

Years ago the *Reader's Digest* asked H. G. Wells to pick the greatest person who ever lived. Wells, a non-Christian, picked Jesus. He said he realized that many people considered Jesus to be "more than a man." But a historian, like himself, has to disregard that fact. He has to treat Jesus as a man, "just as a painter must paint him as a man."

Why did Wells give first place to Jesus? He explains his reason this way:

That place is his by virtue of the . . . profound ideas which he released—the profound importance of the individual under the Fatherhood of God and the conception of the kingdom of heaven. It is one of the most revolutionary changes of outlook that has ever stirred and changed human thought. . . . The historian's test of an individual's greatness is "What did he leave to grow?" Did he start men to thinking along fresh lines with a vigor that persisted after him? By this test Jesus stands first.

What fresh new lines has Jesus started you thinking along since you began meditating on a regular basis? *Speak to Jesus about your desire to grow in your personal relationship with him.*

15

> *"I am the vine, you are the branches.*
> *Whoever remains in me and I in him*
> *will bear much fruit."*   John 15:5

Napoleon said of his leadership charism, "I do, indeed, possess the secret of this magical power that lifts the soul."

Jesus possessed this same power, but to an infinitely greater degree—as Napoleon also admitted. And this is what makes Jesus so different from other leaders.

Other leaders can only inspire us. They can impact us only psychologically. Jesus, on the other hand, can impact us not only psychologically but also mystically.

What does this mean? It means that other leaders can only inflame our emotions and excite our imagination. They can't transfuse us with their own spirit. They can't reach inside us and give us a portion of their own personal power and strength.

Jesus, on the other hand, can do this. He can put his spirit inside us. He can share his power with us. He can enter our minds and our hearts and help us become what we could never become alone.

Recall a time when you experienced the power and spirit of Jesus within you. *Speak to Jesus about how you can open yourself more fully to his transforming power and spirit.*

_____

_____

_____

_____

_____

Day five

"I stand at the door and knock.
If anyone hears my voice
and opens the door,
then I will enter his house
and dine with him."   Revelation 3:20

Paul Stookey won fame with the singing group "Peter, Paul, and Mary." At one point in his career, Paul became dissatisfied with life and turned to the New Testament. He said later:

All the truths I sought were contained in the life of this man. . . . It was fantastic. . . . But it never occurred to me that he could really be the Son of God. . . . I started carrying the Scriptures around with me. . . . It was almost like having a brother with you.

Then Paul met someone backstage at a concert in Austin, Texas. He says:

This guy made all the reading in the Scriptures make sense. . . . So, wow, I started to pray with him, and I asked Jesus to come in and take over my life. And I started to cry and he started to cry. [That day changed my life.]

What role do the Scriptures play in your own life? *Speak to Jesus about how they can begin to nourish your heart and spirit in a more powerful way.*

Day six

Jesus called his disciples to himself,
and from them he chose Twelve,
whom he also named apostles.   Luke 6:13

Someone pointed out (with tongue in cheek) that for simple jobs, like exploring outer space, we choose extraordinary scientists. But for harder jobs, like deciding who's guilty or innocent, we choose ordinary citizens.

Jesus did something similar. When it came to continuing his work on earth, he didn't choose the wise politicians of his time or the powerful rulers of his day. He chose twelve ordinary people. One was Matthew, a tax collector. Another was Simon, a troublemaker. And the others were smelly fishermen.

Jesus knew what he was doing. What we need most in life is not great minds, but great hearts. Not great knowledge, but great dedication. Not great power, but great faith in Jesus, who said:

I do not point to a light for you to see by.
"I am the light."   *John 8:12*
I do not point to a way for you to follow.
"I am the way."   *John 14:6*
I do not point to a life for you to live.
"I am . . . the life."   *John 11:25*

What kind of heart do you have? *Speak to Jesus about how you can open your heart more fully to embrace his transforming presence.*

Day seven

Many of Jesus' followers turned back
and would not go with him any more.
So he asked the twelve disciples,
"And you—would you also like to leave?"
John 6:66–67 (TEV)

The Broadway musical *1776* dealt with those critical days and weeks in our history when our forefathers debated the Declaration of Independence.

At one point in the debate, the fate of our great nation was like a pole standing in wet sand. It could fall either way: backward into the past and continued domination by England, or forward into the future and newfound freedom.

One night John Adams, one of the freedom fighters, was terribly worried about the outcome. Standing all alone in the darkness of Independence Hall, where the great debate was being held, he began to sing in words like these: "Is anyone out there? Does anyone care? Does anyone see what I see?"

These are the same words Jesus is singing today in our darkened world. He's singing all alone, hoping greathearted people will hear him: "Is anyone out there? Does anyone care? Does anyone see what I see?"

Give your own personal answer to Jesus' three questions. *Speak to Jesus about your readiness to join him in his great cause.*

19

3
ANNUNCIATION

Who is Jesus' mother?

"You will conceive in your womb
and bear a son,
and you shall name him Jesus."   Luke 1:31

Mark Twain's story "The Terrible Catastrophe" is about a group of people who get trapped in a terrible situation. They are doomed to die. There is no way they can escape.

Mark Twain didn't want the story to end unhappily, but he didn't see how he could save the people. And so he concluded his story with these two sentences: "I have these characters in such a fix that even I can't get them out of it. Anyone who thinks he can is welcome to try."

The human race was trapped like this thousands of years ago. Sin had entered the world and was spreading out of control, like a wild fire. The human race was doomed. There was no way it could save itself.

God saw the tragic situation and didn't want the story to end sadly. God loved the human race too much for that. So he thought of a way to save it. God decided to send his only Son into the world to become a member of the human race.

God's first step was to find someone to bear his Son. He chose "a virgin betrothed to a man named Joseph, of the house of David, and the virgin's name was Mary." *Luke 1:27*

This week's meditation exercises focus on Mary, the woman who bore Jesus. The grace you ask for in each meditation is this:

Lord, give me knowledge and love
of the mother you chose to bear Jesus.

Conclude each meditation with the prayer that Columbus's sailors prayed nightly during the voyage to America. Each evening at sunset they gathered on deck to sing it.

Hail Holy Queen, mother of mercy,
our life, our sweetness, our hope.
To you we cry, poor banished children of Eve.
To you we direct our sighs,
mourning and weeping in this valley of tears.
Be merciful to us, loving advocate, Virgin Mary,
and after this our exile,
show us your son, Jesus.

Day one

"Behold, I am the handmaid of the Lord.
May it be done to me according to your word."
Luke 1:38

In your imagination, picture the world before the birth of Jesus: people drifting further and further into sin, and evil spreading out of control, like a cancer. Into this world God sent the angel Gabriel.

Coming to Mary, he said, "Hail, favored one! The Lord is with you." But she was greatly troubled at what was said and pondered what sort of greeting this might be.

Then the angel said to her, "Do not be afraid, Mary. . . . You will conceive in your womb and bear a son, and you shall name him Jesus. He will be great and will be called Son of the Most High, and the Lord God will give him the throne of David his father, and . . . of his kingdom there will be no end."

But Mary said to the angel, "How can this be, since I have no relations with a man?" And the angel said to her in reply, "The holy Spirit will come upon you, and the power of the Most High will overshadow you. Therefore the child to be born will be called holy, the Son of God. . . ."

Mary said, "Behold, I am the handmaid of the Lord. May it be done to me according to your word." Then the angel departed from her.   Luke 1:28–35, 38

Reread the passage slowly. *Pause at the end of each paragraph to speak to Mary about what was in her heart at that moment.*

*"He has looked upon his handmaid's lowliness;
behold, from now on
will all ages call me blessed."*   Luke 1:48

A college student was talking to a priest. The conversation drifted to Mary, Jesus' mother. Suddenly the student said, "Let me read you a poem I wrote about Mary." With that, he flipped open a small spiral notebook. The poem went something like this:

*Today I saw a water lily growing in a pond.
It had the freshest yellow color I'd ever seen.
The lily—a precious treasure—
was unconcerned about whether
anyone noticed its astounding beauty.*

*As I sat there,
watching it unfold its petals noiselessly,
I thought of Mary pregnant with Jesus.
She, too, was a precious treasure.
She, too, was unconcerned about whether
anyone noticed her astounding beauty.*

*But to those who did, she shared a secret.
Her beauty came not from herself,
but from the Jesus life within her,
unfolding its petals noiselessly.*

What do you admire most about Mary? *Speak to Mary about the increased role you would like her to play in your life.*

Day three

The Word became flesh and
made his dwelling among us. John 1:14

One hot afternoon in July, seventeen-year-old Joni Eareckson was paralyzed by a diving accident in the Chesapeake Bay. Sadly, doctors confirmed what everyone feared: She would never again move her arms and legs.

Thanks to daily prayer and Bible reading, Joni began to glimpse new possibilities for her life—possibilities she had never dreamed of before the accident. For example, she has since become a skilled painter, holding the brush in her teeth.

One of Joni's favorite paintings portrays Mary receiving the news that she is to become Jesus' mother. Commenting on it, Joni says:

As I sat back and took a long look at the completed picture, I could not help but wonder at this miraculous mystery. God in flesh, Christ incarnate, a divine baby. It is such an astounding miracle that it makes the rest of the miracles in the New Testament almost secondary.

What astounds you most about the way the Son of God entered our world two thousand years ago? *Speak to Mary about her thoughts and feelings before Jesus' birth.*

"The Lord is with you. . . .
Do not be afraid." Luke 1:28, 30

A retreatant had been in psychotherapy for wounds of abuse, received as a child. She wrote to a retreat director:

I had become so turned off to the concept of mothers that I consciously rejected the love of Mary, Jesus' mother. After your talk about personal conversion, I went outside—feeling deeply alone. I prayed for some kind of conversion. I wanted to cry, but haven't for months.

You may have noticed the small round building near the cemetery. Curiosity is one of my strongest traits. So I walked to it and opened the door. When I looked inside, I was filled with fear. There stood a large statue of Mary. My first impulse was to run away in anger. But something drew me slowly to the kneeler at her feet. Then I fell to my knees, weeping into the folds of her robes.

When it was over, I felt cleansed and new. I felt willing to be a trusting child. Even more important, I felt that a mother's love had touched me—leaving in me a true desire to forgive my natural mother.

What childhood wounds of abuse do you still suffer from? *Speak to the compassionate mother of Jesus about them.*

Simeon . . . said to Mary, his mother . . .
"And sorrow, like a sharp sword,
will break your own heart."   Luke 2:34–35 (TEV)

A missionary writes of those South American mothers who must flee political oppression:

Like Mary fleeing with her son to escape Herod's death threat, some will find safety . . . in neighboring nations.

Referring to mothers whose sons were abducted by authorities, the missionary writes:

Mary lost Jesus once. Panic filled her for three days before she found him. Not all mothers are so fortunate. . . . Some of these mothers will never see their children again.

Finally, referring to mothers who hold in their arms the dead body of a son murdered by political enemies, the missionary writes:

When I see Mary holding the lifeless body of her son, I also see those mothers who must repeat that scene in so many ways. . . . If we could hear the anguished hearts of the mothers involved, we would also be able to hear the anguished heart of Mary.
Victor Schymeinsky, Maryknoll magazine

What sorrows of Mary were reflected in your own mother's heart? *Speak to Mary about the sorrows of her own heart.*

Day six

"Nothing will be impossible for God." Luke 1:37

Years ago *The Song of Bernadette* was a best-selling book and a popular film. The story behind the book goes back to World War II.

The Jewish writer Franz Werfel and his wife were fleeing the Nazis. When guards stopped them at the Spanish border, they took shelter in nearby Lourdes, the famous shrine that honors Mary, the mother of Jesus. That night, standing before the shrine, Werfel prayed something like this:

I am not a believer, and I must say so. But in my extreme need, on the chance that I could be wrong about God, I ask him for help for me and my wife.

Werfel returned to the village. Never before, he told a friend later, had he experienced such peace as after that prayer. Within days the couple was able to cross into Spain, board a ship, and sail for America. The first thing Werfel did in America was to write the story of Lourdes and its healing miracles. He called his account *The Song of Bernadette.*

Recall a time when you prayed to the mother of Jesus for help. *Speak to Mary about her motherly concern for you personally.*

Day seven

A great sign appeared in the sky,
a woman clothed with the sun,
with the moon under her feet,
and on her head a crown of twelve stars.

Revelation 12:1

Maryanne Raphael was at Mass with children attending a vacation Bible school. They were singing an old hymn in honor of Mary:

O Queen of heaven, the ocean star,
Guide of the wanderer here below . . .
Save us from peril and from woe.
Mother of Christ, Star of the Sea,
Pray for the wanderer, pray for me.

Suddenly Maryanne heard sobs coming from a shabbily dressed man in a back pew. She checked with the old man to see if he was all right. He replied:

It's just that song. I haven't heard it since I was a little boy. . . . This is the first time in years I've been inside a church. I just came in now to find a place to sit down.

After that, Maryanne saw the man in church regularly, every Sunday.

What role does Jesus' mother play in your understanding of Jesus? *Speak to her about it.*

4
NATIVITY

Why did Jesus become one of us?

*The Word became flesh
and made his dwelling among us.*   John 1:14

John Donne, a seventeenth-century poet, has a story about a man searching for God.

The man is told that God lives atop a tall mountain at the end of the earth. After a long journey the man arrives at the mountain and begins his climb.

About the time the man begins his climb, God says to himself, "What can I do to show my people how much I love them?" He gets the idea to descend the mountain and live among his people as one of them. So he begins descending the mountain.

And so as the man is ascending one side of the mountain, God is descending the other side. They don't see each other because they are on opposite sides of the mountain.

When the man reaches the mountaintop, he is crestfallen to find no one there. He thinks, "God doesn't live here after all." He even begins to think God doesn't exist, saying, "If God doesn't live here, where does he live?"

Donne intended his story for the people of his time. Many of them were searching for God on mountaintops, in deserts, and at the ends of the earth. When they didn't find God, they became discouraged. Like the man in Donne's story, some of them concluded that God doesn't exist. To these people, Donne says:

God doesn't dwell on mountaintops, or in the midst of the desert, or at the ends of the earth. God dwells among his people. He lives in the towns and cities of the world.

This is the great message of the incarnation: God has taken up residence among his people. This week's meditations focus on this incredible message. The grace you ask for in each exercise is this:

Lord, deepen my awareness
of your presence among your people.

During the week ahead, try extra hard to make each meditation come alive in your imagination. For example, in the gospel story in "Day one," imagine you are in the cave with Jesus, Mary, and Joseph. Imagine you are one of the shepherds come to visit Jesus.

Day one

The time came for her to have her child. Luke 2:6

Mary and Joseph went to Bethlehem to register for the census ordered by Emperor Augustus. While there, Jesus was born.

Mary laid him in a manger, because there was no room for them in the inn.

Now there were shepherds . . . keeping the night watch over their flock. . . . The glory of the Lord shone around them, and they were struck with great fear. The angel said to them, "Do not be afraid; for behold, I proclaim to you good news. . . . For today . . . a savior has been born for you who is Messiah and Lord. . . ."
And suddenly there was a multitude of the heavenly host with the angel, praising God and saying: "Glory to God in the highest and on earth peace to those on whom his favor rests."

When the angels went away from them to heaven, the shepherds said to one another, "Let us go, then, to Bethlehem to see this thing that has taken place, which the Lord has made known to us." So they went in haste and found Mary and Joseph, and the infant lying in the manger. Luke 2:7-16

Imagine you are a shepherd who came upon Mary and Joseph just as Jesus was about to be born. You stayed to help. *Experience Jesus' birth before your eyes.*

Day two

God sent his own Son.
He came as the son of a human mother . . .
that we might become God's sons.
Galatians 4:4-5 (TEV)

In the early days of television and plane travel, a young family was outside, on Christmas Day, making a snowman. Suddenly a plane passed overhead. The mother shouted to the children, "That's the plane your uncle is on. Let's all wave. Maybe he'll see us." The children jumped up and down and waved frantically, shouting at the top of their voices.

After the plane had passed over, the tiniest child turned to her father and asked, "Daddy, how do people climb up to the sky to get into the planes?" The father explained that passengers didn't have to climb to the sky to get into planes. The planes came down from the sky to the passengers.

Christmas celebrates the fact that we don't have to climb up to the sky to get to God. God has come down to earth to us. Christmas commemorates that hour when the infinite God of heaven and earth crossed an unimaginable border and took up residence in our world.

Recall your most memorable Christmas. Why do you think Christmas touches your heart so deeply? *Speak to Jesus about the aspect of his birth that moves you most.*

Day three

Who will deliver me from this mortal body?
Thanks be to God
through Jesus Christ our Lord.   Romans 7:24–25

Mud Pie and Dry Leaf were close friends. Both were growing old. Both wanted to go to the holy city of Banaras to bathe in the Ganges River. They believed that if they washed in it, they would be cleansed of all their sins.

The two friends discussed the great distance to be traveled and the hazards to be overcome. They were especially worried about rainstorms and windstorms. So they worked out a plan. Dry Leaf agreed to cover Mud Pie during rainstorms, and Mud Pie agreed to cover Dry Leaf during windstorms.

The first couple of weeks worked find. Mud Pie sat on Dry Leaf during windstorms, and Dry Leaf formed an umbrella over Mud Pie in rainstorms. But then one day a rainstorm and a windstorm struck together. Although the two friends tried their best to help each other, they couldn't. In the end, the wind blew away Dry Leaf and the rain washed away Mud Pie.

How does this parable illustrate your need for God's help, no matter how self-reliant you are or how devoted your friends are to you? *Speak to God about your greatest need for his help at this moment in your life.*

Day four

*"I am the light of the world.
Whoever follows me
will not walk in darkness,
but will have the light of life."* John 8:12

The book *Night Flight* deals with the early years of aviation. It describes the adventures of aviators who used to fly at night, without the aid of radar or radio. The book is not only a fascinating story about night pilots but also a parable of our human situation prior to the coming of Jesus.

Before the Son of God came among us, we lived in a universe that was a deep, dark mystery to us. Worse yet, we were a deep, dark mystery to ourselves. We weren't sure where we came from, where we were going, or how to get to our destination. We were like night fliers, encased in fog and flying through a strange country.

It was into this night-flying situation that Jesus came. He did not take away the fog and the night. He did something more personal. He got into the plane with us. As a result, we are no longer alone in the cockpit, flying blind. We have a copilot sitting beside us.

Do you consult your copilot when the fog rolls in and the nights grow black? Do you trust your copilot? *Speak to Jesus about these things.*

Day five

*Of his own free will he gave up all he had,
and took the nature of a servant.*
Philippians 2:7 (TEV)

An Islamic parable is called "The Watermelon Hunter." It concerns a traveler who strayed into the "Land of the Fools." Outside a village, he saw people fleeing in terror from a field where they were working. They were shouting hysterically, "A monster is in our field!"

The traveler drew nearer and saw that the monster was only a watermelon, a fruit the fools had never seen before. To show how fearless he was, the traveler sliced up the watermelon and ate it. When the villagers saw this, they grew even more terrified. "He's worse than the monster," they said. And they become even more hysterical.

Months later another traveler strayed into the "Land of the Fools," and the same scene repeated itself. This time the traveler didn't play the hero. He took up residence among the fools and taught them to overcome their fear of watermelons. Before he left, the people even cultivated watermelons and ate them.

How is this parable a good illustration of the approach God used with us? Why did God choose this approach? *Speak to Jesus about his own approach to people.*

Day six

We write to you about the Word of life,
which has existed from the very beginning.
We have heard it . . . seen it . . .
and our hands have touched it.   1 John 1:1 (TEV)

Cyril Egan's poem "A Kind of Prayer" describes
a person who is searching frantically for something.
The person searches in the hills, in attics, in cellars,
and in old books. One day a friend asks, "What are
you looking for?" The person responds, "I'm looking
for God." Then the person adds quickly:

Don't tell me I'll find him in my heart
(Though in a sense that's true);
And don't tell me I'll find him
in my fellow man
(Though in a sense that's true, too).
What I'm looking for is a God
making a five-sense breakthrough to humanity.

It is precisely this kind of "breakthrough to
humanity" that God made one star-filled night in
Bethlehem two thousand years ago.

Why do you think the poet is not satisfied with
being told that God can be found in his heart or in his
brothers and sisters? *Speak to God about his decision*
to make a "five-sense breakthrough to humanity."

38

Day seven

"I was . . . a stranger
and you gave me no welcome." Matthew 25:42–43

On Christmas Eve during the Franco-Prussian War in 1870, French and German soldiers were facing each other in trenches, a short distance apart. Suddenly a French soldier began to sing "O Holy Night." He stood on top of the mound of dirt facing the Germans. Not a shot was fired. When the French soldier finished, a German soldier climbed out of his trench and sang "From Heaven to Earth Come." Again, not a shot was fired. Those who witnessed the sight never forgot it.

That brings us to an important point about Christmas. An anonymous poet expressed it in these beautiful words:

When the song of the angels is stilled,
when the star in the sky is gone,
when the kings and princes are home,
when the shepherds are back with the flocks,
the work of Christmas begins:
to find the lost, to heal the broken,
to feed the hungry, to release the prisoner,
to rebuild the nations,
to bring peace among brothers,
to make music with the heart.

Ponder the soldiers' Christmas Eve experience. *Speak to Jesus about how you are taking the poet's point to heart.*

39

5
TWO STANDARDS

Why did Jesus
choose to live as he did?

He emptied himself,
taking the form of a slave. . . .
Because of this, God greatly exalted him
and bestowed on him the name
that is above every name.   Philippians 2:7, 9

During a trip to the Holy Land, James Martin bought a tiny nativity set. The figures were hand-carved from olive wood. When Martin arrived at the Tel Aviv airport for his return trip to the United States, security was tight. The customs officials x-rayed each figure in his nativity set, even the baby Jesus. "We can't take chances," they told Martin. "We've got to make sure there's nothing explosive in that set."

Afterward Martin thought to himself, "If those officials only knew! That set contains the most explosive power in all the world!"

What was Martin thinking about? What is so explosive about the nativity set?

The explosive thing about the nativity set is the message it contains.

This message says that the Son of God chose to enter our world, not as a prince in a mighty palace, but as a pauper in a lowly stable. It says that the Son of God chose to be greeted, not by celebrities, but by smelly shepherds whose status was so low they weren't even allowed to testify in a court of law.

The explosive message of the nativity is that God looks at things in a way that is totally different from the way the world looks at them. Nowhere is this more evident than in the life Jesus chose to live.

He chose poverty: "Foxes have dens and birds . . . have nests, but the Son of Man has nowhere to rest his head." *Luke 9:58* He chose humility: "Learn from me, for I am meek and humble of heart." *Matthew 11:29* He chose dishonor: "The Son of Man . . . must suffer greatly and be rejected by this generation." *Luke 17:24-25*

This set of meditations focuses on Jesus' choice of poverty, humility, and dishonor. The grace you ask for in each meditation is this:

Lord, teach me why you chose
poverty to wealth, humility to pride,
dishonor to honor.

42

Day one

"What profit is there
for one to gain the whole world
and forfeit his life?"   Mark 8:36

In 1923 a meeting took place in Chicago. Attending it were the presidents of the largest steel company, the largest utility company, the largest gas company, the New York Stock Exchange, the Bank of International Settlements, the greatest wheat speculator, the greatest bear on Wall Street, the head of the world's greatest monopoly, and a member of President Harding's cabinet.

Twenty-five years later the president of the steel company, Charles Schwab, had died bankrupt; the president of the utility company, Samuel Insull, had died bankrupt; the president of the gas company, Howard Hobson, had gone insane; the president of the Stock Exchange, Richard Whitney, had just been released from prison; the bank president, Leon Fraser, had died a suicide; the wheat speculator, Arthur Cutten, had died bankrupt; the bear, Jesse Livermore, had died a suicide; the monopoly head, Ivar Kruegar, had died a suicide; the member of the cabinet, Albert Fall, had just been pardoned from prison to die at home.

What lesson might you draw from this true story? Why is this such a hard lesson for people— including yourself—to grasp? *Speak to Jesus about what you can do to apply this lesson to your own life.*

43

*"Where your treasure is,
there also will your heart be."*   Luke 12:34

Former football great O.J. Simpson wrote:

*I sit in my house in Buffalo and sometimes I get
so lonely it's unbelievable. Life has been so good to me.
I've got a great wife, good kids, money, my own
health—I'm lonely and bored. . . . I often wonder why
so many rich people commit suicide. Money sure isn't a
cure-all.*

After fire destroyed his home, Kareem Abdul-
Jabbar, the Los Angeles Lakers star, said:

*My whole perspective changed after the fire. I think
it's more important now for me to spend time with my
son Amir and appreciate other things besides basketball.
There are a lot of things that are more important. Like
friends.*

George Lorimer summed up the point that O.J.
and Kareem are making in these words:

*It's good to have money and the things money can
buy, but it's good, too, to check up once in a while and
make sure you haven't lost the things that money can't
buy.*

How do you deal with loneliness and boredom
when they arise in your life? *Speak to Jesus about the
most important thing in your life that money can't buy.*

Day three

Tombs are their homes forever . . .
though they have called lands
by their names.   Psalm 49:12

Opera star Lily Pons corresponded with royalty, ate barbecue with President Eisenhower, and was received into the French Legion of Honor by Charles de Gaulle.

After Lily Pons died, her estate held an auction. A picture of her at a party with Humphrey Bogart sold for fifty cents. Letters from Princess Grace and Princess Elizabeth went for five dollars.

When you're feeling so important
And your ego is in bloom,
When you simply take for granted
You're the wisest in the room,
When you feel your very absence
Would leave a great big hole,
Just follow these instructions,
They will humble any soul.
Take a bucket filled with water,
Put your hand in to the wrist,
Pull it out, the hole remaining
Is how much you'll be missed.   Anonymous

If someone asked your friends if you had too big an ego, what might they say? *Speak to Jesus about his own ego and what he did to control it.*

45

Day four

"Father . . . not my will but yours be done."
Luke 22:42

Dr. Spence was a popular Protestant minister. His church was always full. But as the years passed, so did his eloquence as a preacher. Understandably, his people began to drift away.

One day the elderly Dr. Spence was keenly aware of his near-empty church. He looked around and then said to those present, "Where are the others who used to worship with us?"

After an embarrassing silence someone said, "There's a new preacher down the street. I think most of them have gone to his church."

Dr. Spence was silent for a moment. Then with a gracious smile he said, "Perhaps it's time to join them." With that, he descended from the pulpit and led his people to the new minister's church.

People aren't touched by someone who smiles graciously in the midst of acceptance, but they are touched mightily by someone who does so in the midst of rejection.

———————

Recall a time when you reacted gracefully after being rejected or passed by. *Speak to Jesus about how he handled rejection and disappointments.*

_____

_____

_____

_____

_____

_____

_____

Day five

*"Everyone who exalts himself will be humbled,
but the one who humbles himself
will be exalted."* Luke 14:11

Everybody knows the cartoon character Charlie Brown. But few people know that he's based on a real person. The real Charlie worked with convicted juvenile delinquents, often housing them temporarily in his own home.

After Charlie died in 1983, a coworker said of him, "He saw his own life as the doing of daily works of charity in imitation of Christ and the saints." The same coworker said that no delinquent who lived with Charlie ever returned to prison. The experience of living with Charlie profoundly affected each one.

Charles Schulz—the Charlie Brown cartoonist— and the real Charlie were good friends. Schulz occasionally offered Charlie a share in the profits from some Charlie Brown spin-off, like T-shirts. But Charlie refused.

Nor did Charlie reveal to people that he was the real Charlie Brown. And to this day, many kids whom Charlie helped have no idea who *really* helped them.

Recall a time when you bragged about yourself or took whatever you could get. *Speak to Jesus about the spirit that motivated the real Charlie Brown.*

*"God resists the proud,
but gives grace to the humble."*   James 4:6

Charles Colson was a top Nixon aide who went to prison in the Watergate scandal. He has since undergone a religious conversion and works full time preaching the Gospel, especially to prisoners.

Colson was deeply influenced by this passage from C. S. Lewis's book *Mere Christianity:*

Pride leads to every other vice: it is the complete anti-God state of mind. . . . As long as you are proud you cannot know God. A proud man is always looking down on things. . . . As long as you are looking down, you cannot see something that is above you.

Commenting on this passage, Colson says, "Suddenly I felt naked and unclean. . . . Lewis's words were describing me." Then he adds, "One passage in particular seemed to sum up what had happened to all of us at the White House: 'Pride is a spiritual cancer: it eats up the very possibility of love, or contentment, or even common sense.' "

How big a problem is pride for you? *Speak to Jesus about what causes your pride.*

Day seven

"No servant can serve two masters." Luke 16:13

The film *Rosemary's Baby* portrays Satan being born into our world, much as Jesus was two thousand years ago. Suppose the movie were true and Satan became incarnate in our world, as Jesus did. What strategy would Satan use to seduce people and get them to follow him?

Saint Ignatius suggests this answer in his meditation on the "Two Standards" (Satan's strategy vs. Christ's strategy).

First, Satan would lead people from a legitimate striving for security to a wrongful striving after money—*wealth*. Second, Satan would lead people from a legitimate striving for acceptance to a wrongful striving for recognition—*honor*. Finally, Satan would lead people from a legitimate appreciation of their self-worth to a sinful indulgence in self-love—*pride*. Thus, Satan's strategy is to seduce people gradually, leading them from legitimate self-striving to sinful self-indulgence.

Christ's strategy is to protect people from Satan's strategy by inviting them to imitate his own spirit of personal detachment from wealth, honor, and pride.

How strong a hold does the attraction for wealth and recognition have on you? *Speak to Jesus about what you might do to diminish that hold.*

6

THREE CLASSES OF PERSONS

Are you free enough to follow Jesus?

> *When the young man heard this statement,*
> *he went away sad,*
> *for he had many possessions.*   Matthew 19:22

In *Winning by Letting Go,* Elizabeth Brenner tells how people in rural India catch monkeys.

First they cut a hole in a box. Then they put a tasty nut in the box. The hole is just big enough for the monkey to put its hand through. But once the monkey clutches the nut, its fist is too big to withdraw. So the monkey has two choices. It can release the nut and go free, or it can hang on to it and stay trapped. Monkeys often elect to hang on to the nut.

The situation of the monkey is not unlike our own situation when it comes to following Jesus. We want to do it, but at the same time we often want to hold on to something that keeps us from doing it. In other words, the nut in the monkey's hand stands for something we must let go of if we want to follow Jesus as we should.

This week's meditations deal with this dilemma. They try to help you determine if you are free enough to let go of material wealth and personal ambition for the sake of a greater good or a larger cause. The grace you ask for in each meditation is the following:

Lord, help me let go of
whatever keeps me from following you.

This week's meditations are immensely important. You may wish to ask God's special help by doing some extra service for others or by making some personal sacrifice, like giving up eating between meals.

Be especially faithful in discerning and recording whatever insights, resolutions, or feelings God may put into your heart. Don't go into great detail. Two or three short lines will do. For example, you may simply write:

Week 6, Day one
   The "pearl" in my life that I need to let go of is worrying about what my friends think of me. I'm more concerned about their approval than I am about God's plan for me. That's crazy.

Now begin. Keep in mind that God can fill your heart with himself only to the extent that you open your heart to God.

Day one

> *"If your right eye causes you to sin,*
> *tear it out and throw it away.*
> *It is better for you to lose one of your members*
> *than to have your whole body*
> *thrown into Gehenna."*   Matthew 5:29

One day a poor peasant boy was walking along a beach. Seeing something glittering in the sand, he bent down and picked it up. It was a huge, beautiful pearl.

The boy was beside himself with joy. He knew that his worries were over. He'd never have to work again in his life. But when the boy went to the pearl dealers, they offered him such a small sum that he knew he was being cheated. He refused to sell it.

In the days that followed, the boy was attacked several times. The pearl buyers were out to get his pearl, even if it meant killing him. It was now clear that if he wanted to save his life, he must give up his pearl.

The next morning, with the pearl dealers looking on, the boy went down to the beach and threw his pearl as far as he could out into the sea.

Then the boy left the beach, proud of himself and at peace with the world. He knew he had become a man that day, because he let go of something precious to preserve something even more precious.

Is there a "pearl" in your life that you need to let go of if you want to follow Jesus and live out God's plan for you? *Speak to Jesus about it.*

53

Day two

As high as the heavens are above the earth,
so high are my ways above your ways
and my thoughts above your thoughts.   Isaiah 55:9

Bill Havens was a member of the American canoe team scheduled to compete in the 1924 Olympics. In those days there was no jet travel across the ocean. Thus when the doctor said Bill's wife would have their baby sometime during the games, Bill hesitated to go to Paris.

His wife urged him to go, assuring him that she would be fine. But Bill felt his place was with her. He gave up his place on the team. A few days before his wife gave birth to their son, Frank, the team won the canoe competition.

Bill never mentioned his disappointment over missing out on the Olympics. Years passed; then came July 1952. One day a cable arrived for Bill. It was from Helsinki, Finland, where the Olympics were in progress. It read: "Dad, I won. I'm bringing home the gold medal you lost while waiting for me to be born." Bill's son, Frank, had just won the Olympic singles canoe competition.

Recall a time when you said no to something you wanted and yes to duty, as Bill Havens did. *Speak to Jesus about how the decision helped you grow.*

Day three

*"Whoever loses his life for my sake
and that of the gospel will save it."* Mark 8:35

George Burns made a film called *Oh, God!* He played the part of God and wore thick glasses and a funny little hat. John Denver played a supermarket employee.

One day God appeared to the employee with a message for the people of the world. The employee agreed to communicate it as best he could. That's when his problems began.

Getting people to take him seriously turned out to be next to impossible. Soon the supermarket employee found himself on the verge of losing his job. Completely frustrated, he turned to God and said, "Preaching your word is costing me my job!"

God was unimpressed. He simply said, "That's not a bad trade, is it? Lose your job and save the world."

It's so easy to get lost in our own little world and to see only our own problems. It's so easy to think only of ourselves and not to think of the greater good of everyone.

Do you really believe that the only things people keep in life are those they are willing to give away? *Talk to God about your readiness to sacrifice your personal desires and dreams for the greater good of all.*

Day four

"I will always go with you wherever you go, even if it means death." 1 Samuel 15:21 (TEV)

Abraham Lincoln knew failure. For thirty years it dogged his every footstep. It walked the streets with him during the day and went to bed with him at night. A partial list of his failures reads as follows:

1832   was defeated for the legislature
1833   failed in business
1836   suffered a nervous breakdown
1843   lost the nomination for Congress
1854   was defeated for the Senate
1856   lost the vice presidential bid

When he was elected president in 1860, Lincoln was prepared for the frustrations he had to contend with during the Civil War years. Another man might have collapsed under the ordeal. Not Lincoln. He had learned to say yes to whatever God had chosen for him: sickness over health, poverty over wealth, dishonor over honor.

On Good Friday, 1863, Lincoln said yes to the final choice: a short life over a long one. He was assassinated.

How reluctant are you—right now—to say yes to the things Lincoln did? *Speak to Jesus about what you might do to diminish that reluctance.*

Day five

"The seeds that fell on rocky ground
stand for those who hear the message
and receive it gladly.
But it does not sink deep into them; . . .
when the time of testing comes, they fall away."
Luke 8:13 (TEV)

Two brothers, Clarence and Robert, committed their lives to Jesus in their youth.

Clarence grew up and became a civil rights activist. Working for civil rights was not a popular occupation in the South in the 1960s. Tension between blacks and whites was high. People staged sit-ins in restaurants. Marchers paraded down city streets. Police used dogs and fire hoses to disperse black protestors and white sympathizers.

Clarence's brother, Robert, grew up and became a lawyer. One day Clarence asked Robert for legal help in a civil rights matter. Robert refused, saying it could hurt his political future. Clarence was stunned. He confronted Robert about his commitment to Jesus. Robert responded, saying, "I do follow Jesus, but not to the cross. I'm not getting myself crucified."

Clarence looked at his brother and said, "Robert, you're not a follower of Jesus; you're only one of his fans."

In what sense are you more of a fan of Jesus than a follower? *Speak to Jesus about the steps you could begin to take to become a full-fledged follower.*

_____

_____

_____

_____

Day six

"I was hungry and you gave me food . . .
a stranger and you welcomed me,
naked and you clothed me." Matthew 25:35–36

A king had no one to succeed him. So he invited qualified young people to be interviewed by him, with a view to being his successor.

A poverty-stricken young man felt an inner call to apply, but he had nothing to wear for the interview and no money to buy food and clothing for the long journey. He decided to work night and day to earn the needed money. When all was ready, he set out.

One day, after weeks of hard travel, the young man caught sight of the king's castle on a high hill in the distance. About the same time, however, he saw a beggar sitting at the side of the road. Shivering and cold, the beggar said in a weak voice, "Help me, I am dying!"

The young man gave the beggar his good clothes and all the money and provisions he had. Then, with fearful heart, he continued his journey to the castle in the beggar's clothes and with no money for his return trip home.

When the young man appeared before the king, he was shocked. Seated on the throne was the beggar, wearing the clothes he had given him. The beggar turned out to be the king himself.

What is the point of this story? *Speak to Jesus about the difficulty you have in applying it to your life.*

Day seven

"A man gave a great dinner
to which he invited many. . . .
But one by one,
they all began to excuse themselves."
Luke 14:16, 18

In one of his classic meditation exercises, Saint Ignatius describes "Three Classes of Persons."

All three classes want to follow Jesus more closely. But all three are attached to something that threatens to keep them from doing this.

The *first* class of persons is the *dreamer* class. They admit the problem. They see the danger. But they love their attachment too much to give it up. So they do nothing about it.

The *second* class is the *dodger* class. They admit the problem. They also see the danger. And they also love their attachment too much to give it up. They are willing, however, to guard against the danger. For example, they will pray daily that it won't keep them from following Jesus.

The *third* class is the *doer* class. They admit their problem. They also see the danger. They also love their attachment. But unlike the other two classes, they are willing to give up the attachment if, after prayer, this is what God seems to want them to do.

What attachment do you have that threatens to keep you from following Jesus more perfectly? *Speak to Jesus about it.*

7
THREE KINDS OF HUMILITY

How much do you love God?

"Love the Lord, your God,
with all your heart, with all your being,
with all your strength,
and with all your mind."   Luke 10:27

An angel was walking down the street. In the angel's right hand was a torch; in its left hand was a bucket of water. "What are you going to do with that torch and that bucket of water?" someone asked. The angel said:

With the torch, I'm going to burn down the mansions of heaven; and with the bucket of water, I'm going to put out the fires of hell. Then we're going to see who really loves God.

The point of the story is that many people keep the commandments, not out of love of God, but out of fear of hell or hope of heaven.

The meditation exercises that follow focus on the love of God. This love operates on three levels, as

Saint Ignatius notes in his meditation on the "Three Kinds of Humility."

The first level is the *minimal* level. At this level, the lover loves God at least this much: There's no person or thing on earth so attractive that for that person or that thing the lover would offend God seriously.

The first level of love is summed up this way in Saint Ignatius' "Prayer for Generosity":

Lord,
teach me to be generous.
Teach me to serve you as you deserve;
to give and not to count the cost;
to fight and not to heed the wounds;
to toil and not to seek for rest;
to labor and not to ask for reward,
except to know
that I am doing your will.

The second level of love, the *logical* level, is a higher level. At this level, the lover isn't content with not offending the beloved. The lover wants to do more. The lover is impatient to please the beloved.

The second level of love is summed up this way in Saint Ignatius' "*Suscipe*":

Take, O Lord,
and receive all my liberty,
my memory, my understanding, and all my will,
whatsoever I have and possess.

All these things you have given to me.
All these things, O Lord,
I now place totally at your service.

All are yours to do with as you wish.
Assure me only of your love and your grace.
These will be enough for me.

The third level of love is the most perfect level. It has been called the *folly* level, because this level of love seems like madness to the nonlover. Concretely, at this level, the lover desires to be exactly like the beloved.

Thus the follower of Jesus prefers poverty to wealth, because Jesus was poor. The follower also prefers dishonor to honor, because Jesus was dishonored. And finally, the follower prefers to be regarded foolish by worldly standards, rather than wise, because Jesus was looked upon that way.

Saint Ignatius sums up the third level of love with this prayer:

Lord,
I ask to serve you:
first,
in the highest degree of poverty of spirit
—even actual material poverty—
if it pleases you;
and second,
in bearing insults and reproaches,
in order to resemble Jesus more closely,
providing this can be done without sin
on anyone's part and that you wish it for me.

The grace you ask for in each meditation exercise is always the same. It is expressed this way in the show-stopping song "Day by Day" from the Broadway musical *Godspell:*

Lord,
"May I know you more clearly,
Love you more dearly,
And follow you more nearly,
Day by day."

You might wish to end each meditation exercise this week with this poetic prayer that Saint Ignatius was fond of:

Soul of Christ, sanctify me.
Body of Christ, save me.
Blood of Christ, inebriate me.

Water from the side of Christ, wash me.
Passion of Christ, strengthen me.
O Good Jesus, hear me.
Within thy wounds hide me.
Permit me not to be separated from thee.
From the wicked foe defend me.
At the hour of death call me
and bid me come to thee,
that with all the saints I may praise thee
for ever and ever.
Amen.

Day one

*"No one who sets a hand to the plow
and looks to what was left behind
is fit for the kingdom of God."* Luke 9:62

Someone once said that disciples come in three varieties: tugboats, sailboats, and rafts.

Tugboats follow Jesus not only in sunny weather but also in stormy weather. They follow him not only when the wind and the waves serve them but also when they oppose them. They are people who love not only when they feel like it but always, because Jesus said, "Love one another as I love you." *John 15:12*

Sailboat disciples follow Jesus only in sunny weather. They go in his direction only when the wind and the waves serve them. When stormy weather comes, they tend to go in the direction they are blown. In short, they follow the crowd more than they follow Jesus.

Finally, there are raft disciples. They are not really followers of Jesus at all. They won't even follow him when the wind and the waves serve them. They go in his direction only when they are pulled or pushed. They act like Christians not because they want to but because they have to or because it is to their personal advantage to do so.

What kind of a disciple are you? *Speak to Jesus about whatever threatens to keep you from following him in stormy weather.*

Day two

*"Everyone who acknowledges me before others
I will acknowledge."* Matthew 10:32

Arthur Jones was drafted into the British Royal
Air Force. The first night in camp he had to make a
decision. Should he continue to kneel for his night
prayers, as he had always done at home?

He squirmed a little bit. Then he thought to
himself, "Why should I change just because people
are watching? Now that I'm away from home, am I
going to let other people dictate my actions?"

Arthur knelt. By the time he finished, he was
aware that everyone noticed him. And when he made
the Sign of the Cross, he was aware that everyone
knew he was Catholic.

As it turned out, he was the only Catholic in the
barracks. Yet night after night he knelt. He said later
that those ten minutes on his knees often sparked
serious discussions that lasted for hours.

On the last night in boot camp, someone said,
"You're the finest Christian I've ever met." Arthur
disagreed, but thanked the person anyway.

How much are your actions affected by what
others may think of you? *Speak to Jesus about what
enabled him to be unaffected by what others thought.*

Day three

*"The Father will honor
whoever serves me."* John 12:26

The film *Chariots of Fire* is based on the true
story of Eric Liddell, England's top 100-meter runner
and favorite to win the 1924 Olympics.

Being deeply religious, Eric never ran on Sunday.
Then came the bombshell. When the Olympic
schedule was released, the final for the 100-meter
event was scheduled to be run on Sunday. Eric was
crestfallen.

When word got around England that Eric
wouldn't run on Sunday, incredible pressure was put
upon him to violate his conscience. Eric refused to
yield. English newspapers even called him a traitor
to his country, but Eric still remained loyal to his
beliefs. Eventually Eric switched to the 400-meter
event, a race he had never run in his life.

According to the movie, just before the race, the
American runner, Jackson Scholz, handed Eric a note.
It contained this sentence: "The Father will honor
whoever serves me." *John 12:26* Seconds later Eric
won the 400-meter event. Still clutched in his hand
was the note Jackson Scholz had given him.

Recall a time when you were pressured to violate
your conscience. How vulnerable are you to such
pressure? *Contemplate the reward that awaits those
who remain faithful to their conscience.*

Day four

The attitude you should have is the one
that Christ Jesus had. . . .
He gave up all he had,
and took the nature of a servant.
Philippians 2:5, 7 (TEV)

A powerful king fell in love with a peasant girl. But kings never married peasants; they married only royalty. This king, however, was so powerful that he knew he could marry the girl and get away with it.

But another thought occurred to the king. If he married the peasant girl and stayed a king, there might always be something essential missing in their relationship. The gap between them might be too great. She might always be conscious of the fact that he was royalty and she was merely a lowly peasant.

So the king decided to resign his kingship and become a lowly peasant himself. Then he would offer the girl his love as one lowly peasant to another. The king realized, however, that this plan could backfire. If people considered him a fool for having done what he did, the girl might reject him. He could end up losing both his love and his throne.

But the king decided that he loved the peasant girl so much that he would risk everything to make true love between them possible.

How is this story a parable about Jesus? How willing are you to risk all to follow Jesus? *Speak to Jesus about how to overcome your fears to do this.*

Day five

Jesus rebuked Peter and said,
"Get behind me, Satan.
You are thinking not as God does,
but as human beings do." Mark 8:33

A Man for All Seasons tells the true story of Sir Thomas More.

In a dramatic scene from the play, More's friend Lord Norfolk tries to persuade Sir Thomas to sign a document declaring that he thinks the recent marriage of King Henry VIII is valid. If More doesn't sign, the king will execute him for treason.

More doesn't think the marriage is valid and refuses to compromise his conscience. Lord Norfolk grows impatient, saying:

Oh confound all this. . . . Frankly I don't know whether the marriage is lawful or not. But damn it, Thomas, look at those names. . . . You know these men! Can't you do what I did and come with us for fellowship?

Sir Thomas still refuses to sign. To the dismay of his political friends and associates, he puts his love for God before all other loves, even his love for himself. Some considered him mad.

To what extent are you being pressured not to follow Jesus? Is this pressure exerted more by friends than by enemies? *Speak to Jesus about how he handled such pressure.*

Day six

"No one has greater love than this,
to lay down one's life
for one's friends." John 15:13

Colonel John Mansure of Florida's Patrick Air Force Base heard this story and wrote it up for *Missileer* magazine.

Several rounds of mortar landed on a Vietnam orphanage, wounding several of the children. An American navy doctor arrived on the scene and saw that one of the girls needed an immediate blood transfusion.

Quickly, several unharmed children were tested to see if they had the right blood type. Using pidgin Vietnamese, the doctor explained to the eligible children the need for the blood and asked if anyone would give it.

At first no one responded. Then a small boy slowly raised his hand. The doctor immediately swabbed the boy's arm with alcohol, inserted the needle, and withdrew the blood. After it was all over, the boy began to cry. No amount of hugging would comfort him.

Later it was discovered why. The boy had misunderstood that by giving his blood, he himself would die. When asked why he gave his blood anyway, he said, "The girl was my friend."

How ready are you to love Jesus as he loved you—even to giving up all, even your life, for him? *Speak to Jesus about your fear of going this far.*

Day seven

Thomas answered and said to Jesus,
"My Lord and my God!" John 20:28

Piri Thomas was a convict, a drug addict, and an attempted killer. One night he felt an overwhelming desire to pray. But he was sharing his cell with another prisoner called "the thin kid." So he waited until the kid was asleep. Then he got out of bed, knelt on the cold concrete, and prayed aloud. He writes:

I told God what was in my heart. . . . I talked to him plain . . . no big words. . . . I talked to him of my wants and lacks, of my hopes and disappointments. . . . I felt like I could even cry . . . something I hadn't been able to do for years.

After Piri finished his prayer, a voice said, "Amen." It was "the thin kid." "There we were," Piri said, "he lying down, head on bended elbows, and I still on my knees." No one spoke for a long time. Then the kid whispered, "I believe in *Dios* also."

The two young men talked a long time. Then Piri climbed back into his bunk. "Good night, Chico," he said. "I'm thinking that God is always with us. It's just that we aren't always with him."

How ready are you to turn your life over to God—right now—as Piri did? *Speak to Jesus about this from the heart, as Piri did.*

71

8
BAPTISM AND TEMPTATIONS

Why was Jesus baptized and tempted?

*Crowds . . . came out
to be baptized by John.*   Luke 3:7

Not far from the Dead Sea there is a shallow spot in the Jordan River. From earliest times it has been used as a crossing for caravans from all over the Near East. On an afternoon, one could see Arabs with white head coverings, Babylonians with rings in their noses, and Ethiopians with shiny, ebony-colored skin. It was a favorite place for people to gather to exchange world news.

One day, however, a new attraction sent people flocking to the shallow crossing. For weeks there had been rumors of a strange figure preaching there. He was dressed like the prophets of old, wearing clothes made of camel's hair with a leather belt around his waist. His name was John and his message was simple: "Turn away from your sins and be baptized." *Luke 3:3 (TEV)*

John's expression "turn away from your sins" translates the Hebrew word that means "to return from traveling down a wrong road and to set out anew on the right road." In other words, people should admit their sinful ways and correct them.

One day John was taken by surprise by something he hadn't expected. There wading through the water to be baptized was Jesus. What should he do? John tried to get Jesus to change his mind, saying, " 'I need to be baptized by you, and yet you are coming to me?' Jesus said to him in reply, 'Allow it now.' " *Matthew 3:14-15* And so Jesus was baptized like the rest of the people.

This week's meditations focus on Jesus' baptism— and his temptations in the desert, which followed immediately after his baptism. The grace you ask for is the same as last week's grace.

Lord,
"May I know you more clearly,
Love you more dearly,
And follow you more nearly,
Day by day."

*While Jesus was praying, heaven was opened
and the holy Spirit descended upon him
in bodily form like a dove.
And a voice came from heaven,
"You are my beloved Son;
with you I am well pleased."*   Luke 3:21-22

Ancient peoples viewed the universe as three worlds stacked up on top of one another. The top world was where God lived; the middle one was where the human race lived; and the bottom world was where dead people went.

Following the sin of Adam and Eve, the middle world became more and more evil. Holy people prayed to God to come down from his world and clean up the mess in their world: "LORD, tear the sky open and come down." *Psalm 144:5 (TEV)*

It is against this background that the description of Jesus' baptism must be interpreted. First, the sky opens. In the light of what was just said, the meaning of this event is clear. What people asked God to do is now happening: God is tearing open the sky. God is coming down from his world to clean up the mess in their world. In other words, Jesus' baptism marks the dawn of a "new era" in human history.

Imagine you are present at Jesus' baptism. Experience it with all five of your senses. *Speak to Jesus about the practical meaning his baptism has for you.*

Day two

*The holy Spirit descended upon Jesus
in bodily form like a dove.*   Luke 3:22

After the sky opened above the waters of the
Jordan, the Holy Spirit descended like a dove and
hovered over Jesus.

This event recalls the dawn of creation, when
God's power hovered over the water like a dove. The
Bible says, "In the beginning . . . the power of God
was moving over the water. Then God commanded,
'Let there be light'—and light appeared." *Genesis 1:1-3
(TEV)*

Jewish rabbis first likened God's power "moving
over the water" to a dove. Luke chose this same image
to teach that Jesus' baptism begins a "new" creation.
God is about to fulfill his promise to Isaiah: "I am
about to create . . . a new earth; the things of the past
shall not be remembered or come to mind. Instead,
there shall always be rejoicing and happiness in what
I create." *Isaiah 65:17-18*

And so the "new era" that begins with Jesus'
baptism is a "new creation" of our world. Jesus is the
one who will set in motion the re-creation of our
world, which sin nearly destroyed. He is the one who
will set in motion God's kingdom on earth.

What kind of role are you currently playing in
the re-creation of the world? *Speak to the Holy Spirit
about what role you could begin to play.*

Day three

"This is my beloved Son." Matthew 3:17

After the sky opened above Jesus, and after the Holy Spirit descended upon him, a voice from heaven said, "This is my beloved Son."

The voice identifies Jesus as the Son of God. It reveals Jesus as the "new Adam," the firstborn of the "new creation." Commenting on Jesus as the "new Adam," Paul writes:

The first man [Adam] was from the earth, earthly; the second man [Jesus], from heaven. . . . Just as we have borne the image of the earthly one [the old Adam], we shall also bear the image of the heavenly one [the new Adam]. 1 Corinthians 15:47–49

Paul's words remind us that we are citizens of two worlds. We bear the likeness of both the first Adam and the second Adam.

We have within our beings parts of both Adams. We experience the pull of the flesh of the first Adam and the pull of the Spirit of the second Adam. This explains why, at times, we experience spiritual conflict: a pull toward good and a pull toward evil.

How do you handle spiritual conflict when it comes? *Speak to Jesus about how he handled spiritual conflict in his life.*

Day four

Jesus was led by the Spirit
into the desert
to be tempted by the devil.   Matthew 4:1

Jesus fasted for forty days . . . and afterwards he
was hungry. The tempter approached and said to him,
"If you are the Son of God, command that these stones
become loaves of bread." He said in reply, "It is written:
'One does not live by bread alone, but by every word that
comes forth from the mouth of God.' "
   Then the devil took him to the holy city, and made
him stand on the parapet of the temple, and said to
him, "If you are the Son of God, throw yourself down.
For it is written: 'He will command his angels
concerning you, and with their hands they will support
you, lest you dash your foot against a stone.' " Jesus
answered him, "Again it is written, 'You shall not put
the Lord, your God, to the test.' "
   Then the devil took him up to a very high
mountain, and showed him all the kingdoms of the
world in their magnificence, and he said to him, "All
these I shall give to you, if you will prostrate yourself
and worship me." At this, Jesus said to him, "Get away,
Satan! It is written: 'The Lord, your God, shall you
worship and him alone shall you serve.' " Then the
devil left him.   Matthew 4:2-11

Imagine you are present in the desert with Jesus.
Picture the devil as a shadow falling across the sand.
Pause after each temptation and ask Jesus how it applies
to your life.

*"If you are the Son of God,
command that these stones
become loaves of bread."* Matthew 4:3

Jesus' temptations show that he felt the same inner tension between flesh and spirit that we feel. He experienced the same inner conflict between right and wrong that we experience. In other words, his temptations show that he was *truly human,* just as we are.

Jesus' temptations show something else. They show that Jesus reacted to the devil in a totally different way than we do. He did not hesitate or waver. No one ever showed such firmness in the face of temptation. In other words, Jesus' reaction to temptation shows that he is more than just another human. There is something very special about him.

The devil gives us a clue to this "specialness" when he says to Jesus, "If you are the *Son of God.*" Jesus is not just another human being. He is *God's Son* become man. Years later Paul would describe Jesus this way: "He was in the form of God . . . coming in human likeness and found human in appearance." *Philippians 2:6-7*

And so Jesus' temptations point to his identity. He is more than just another man. He is God's Son, clothed in flesh and blood.

What is the source of most of your temptations? *Speak to Jesus about how he handled his temptations.*

Day six

It is written,
"The first man, Adam, became a living being,"
the last Adam a life-giving spirit.   1 Corinthians 15:45

Jesus' temptations point not only to his *identity* but also to his *mission* on earth.

Recall that after the first creation the devil tempted Adam, the first man, and led him into sin. That sin brought spiritual death to all Adam's descendants. Paul writes in his Letter to the Romans, "Through one person sin entered the world, and through sin, death." *Romans 5:12*

Now the devil repeats the process. He tempts Jesus, the first man of the "new" creation, to get him to sin, also. But Jesus stands firm and is victorious.

Jesus' victory points to the *mission* his Father gave him. Paul describes it this way: "Just as through one transgression condemnation came upon all, so through one righteous act acquittal and life came to all." *Romans 5:18*

In other words, Jesus' *mission* on earth is to restore to the human race the life it lost through Adam's sin. Elsewhere Paul describes Jesus' mission this way: "Just as in Adam all die, so too in Christ shall all be brought to life." *1 Corinthians 15:22*

What are you doing to nourish and strengthen the bond of your union with Christ? *Speak to Jesus about what else you might do.*

*"The Son of Man did not come to be served
but to serve and to give his life
as a ransom for many."* Mark 10:45

Jesus' temptations preview the life-style he will follow in carrying out his mission.

First, Jesus' refusal to turn stone into bread shows that he will not use his marvelous power for his own personal comfort or benefit. Rather, Jesus will sweat, hunger, and suffer to accomplish his work on earth.

Second, Jesus' refusal to throw himself down from the Temple and let the angels protect him previews that he hasn't come to be served but to serve. Later he will tell his disciples, "Whoever wishes to be first among you will be the slave of all. For the Son of Man did not come to be served but to serve." *Mark 10:44-45*

Finally, Jesus' refusal to kneel before the devil—even in exchange for the whole world—previews that he will not compromise or negotiate with evil. The temptation implies, correctly, that at that moment the world belonged to the devil to give to whomever he wished. Jesus' refusal shows that God is God, right is right, wrong is wrong. Jesus will suffer—even die—at the hands of evil, rather than negotiate with it.

How are you, perhaps, compromising with evil in your life? *Speak to Jesus about what steps you might take to change this situation.*

9
SERMON ON THE MOUNT

How blessed are you?

His disciples came to him.
He began to teach them.   Matthew 5:1

Tom Dooley captured the imagination of the world in the 1950s. Fresh out of medical school and the navy, he went to Asia to do medical work among the very poor. This was especially surprising because Dooley came from a wealthy family and enjoyed the good life. Commenting on this in *Guideposts* magazine, he says:

If people can be born with a desire, I guess mine was to have a good time, and good times came easy in our home. There was plenty of money; I had my own horse, went to school abroad, studied to be a concert pianist.

But Dooley's family was also deeply religious. He says:

We were the prayingest family you ever saw. We prayed when we got up in the morning, when we sat down to eat, when we finished eating, when we went to bed, and frequently in between.

Tom Dooley's family also read the Bible. Tom's own favorite reading was the Beatitudes in the Sermon on the Mount. Dooley says:

I loved the Beatitudes because they talked about what I was interested in. "Blest" means "happy," and that's just what I wanted to be. Here were the rules for happiness.

The meditation exercises for this week focus on the Beatitudes in Jesus' Sermon on the Mount. The grace you ask for is:

Lord, help me take to heart
your teaching on the Beatitudes.

During the week, you might wish to read the following passages from the Sermon on the Mount. As you do, imagine yourself sitting on the mount with hundreds of people. Some are lame; some are blind; some are old. Watch the expressions on their faces as Jesus talks.

The Beatitudes	Matthew 5:1–12
Salt and light	Matthew 5:13–16
Judging others	Matthew 7:1–6
The house builders	Matthew 7:24–27

Day one

*"Blessed are they who mourn,
for they will be comforted."*   Matthew 5:4

Tom Dooley's inspiration to work among Asia's poor came one day when he was in the navy.

His ship picked up a thousand refugees drifting off the coast of Vietnam. Tom plunged into the backbreaking job of helping these people. He discovered that the simplest medical treatment brought smiles to their pain-filled faces. He also discovered that helping them made him happier than he'd ever been in his life.

When Tom's hitch in the navy was over, he went back to Asia to continue helping these poor people. Volunteers flocked to join him.

One day he was talking with a coworker about the Beatitudes, especially his favorite: "Blessed are they who mourn." He explained that for him the word *mourn* didn't mean "to be unhappy." It meant "to be more aware of sorrow in our world than of pleasure."

"If you're extrasensitive to sorrow," Tom said, and try to alleviate it, "you can't help but be happy. That's just the way it is."

Are you more aware of sorrow in our world than of pleasure? *Speak to Jesus about what you might begin to do to alleviate some of that sorrow.*

_____

_____

_____

_____

_____

_____

_____

Day two

*"Blessed are the poor in spirit;
for theirs is the kingdom of heaven."*   Matthew 5:3

Years ago there was a movie called *Quo Vadis*. It starred Deborah Kerr and dealt with the persecution of Christians in ancient Rome.

One day, after a dangerous filming session, a reporter asked Deborah, "Weren't you afraid when the lions rushed you in the arena?"

Deborah replied, "Not at all! I'd read the script, and I knew I'd be rescued."

This is the kind of childlike trust that "poor people" had in God in Jesus' time. The Hebrew word for these "poor people" was *ani*. It referred to those people who were economically and politically helpless. People in this situation became *detached from material things* and *attached to God*.

Thus, the "poor in spirit," whom Jesus says are blessed, are those people who have come to realize that they can't depend on material things for happiness. And so they seek their happiness in God alone. God means everything to them; material things mean next to nothing. These people are, as Jesus said, truly "blessed."

What is your most valuable possession? Why do you tend to find your happiness more in things than in God? *Speak to Jesus about your answer, and listen carefully to his response to you.*

_____

_____

_____

_____

Day three

"Blessed are the peacemakers,
for they will be called children of God."
Matthew 5:9

An elderly couple had a problem. Children were cutting across a corner of their lawn, wearing an ugly path through it.

At first the children merely annoyed the couple. But after a while the couple's annoyance turned to anger. The couple knew something had to be done. The situation was poisoning their attitude toward the children and destroying their peace of mind.

The couple hit upon a solution. They put crushed gravel on the path. Then they lined it with flowers. After that, they set a bench on the edge of the path. On afternoons when school let out, the couple sat on the bench and greeted the children as they came by.

The response of the children was amazing. They stopped and thanked the couple for the path. They even asked the names of the flowers and, sometimes, they sat down to talk to the couple. In short, the couple turned an unhappy situation into a happy one.

As a rule, do you try to handle ugly situations in a peaceful, creative way, as the couple did? *Speak to Jesus about a potentially ugly situation in your life right now.*

Day four

*"Blessed are the merciful,
for they will be shown mercy."* Matthew 5:7

Two men greeted each other warmly in Tokyo's International Airport. Both had tears in their eyes. The last time they met was forty years earlier as enemies in an Okinawan cave. At that time, the American, Sergeant Ponich, was holding a child in his arms. The five-year-old had been shot through both legs. Suddenly the Japanese, Ishiboshi, leaped out of the darkness and pointed his rifle at Ponich, prepared to shoot.

There wasn't a thing Ponich could do. He simply placed the child on the ground, took out his canteen, and began to wash the boy's wounds. Ishiboshi watched in amazement and then lowered his rifle. When Ponich had finished, he cradled the child in his arms, bowed to Ishiboshi in gratitude, and took the child to an American field hospital.

How did the two men happen to meet after all those years? In 1985 Ponich wrote a letter to a Tokyo newspaper, thanking the soldier who mercifully spared his life forty years before. Ishiboshi saw the letter and contacted the paper. The paper then arranged the memorable airport meeting.

What are some opportunities you have right now for showing mercy to others? *Speak to Jesus about these opportunities, recalling his promise, "Blessed are the merciful, for they will be shown mercy."*

Day five

*"Blessed are you when they insult you
and persecute you . . . because of me."*
Matthew 5:11

Martin Niemoller was a German submarine commander during World War I. For his service to his country, he was awarded the Iron Cross. After the war he studied for the ministry and was ordained.

Before the outbreak of World War II, Niemoller backed the Nazi party. But when he saw the direction the party began to take, he broke with it and denounced it publicly. He was immediately arrested and sent to the Dachau concentration camp. Miraculously, he survived eight years of imprisonment.

Upon his release after World War II, Niemoller became active in the world peace movement. One day, while speaking at a German university, he was heckled and insulted by a crowd of 1,200 students for publicly asking pardon of the Jews.

Instead of growing angry at the insults, Niemoller imitated the disciples of Jesus, who rejoiced "that they had been found worthy to suffer dishonor for the sake of the name." *Acts 5:41*

Recall a time when you reacted well when someone insulted you. *Speak to Jesus about how he handled insults and heckling so well, especially on the cross.*

Day six

*"Blessed are they who hunger and thirst
for righteousness,
for they will be satisfied."*   Matthew 5:6

Therese Martin was a nineteenth-century saint. At the age of fifteen, she entered the Carmelite convent in Lisieux, France. From her first days inside the big red brick building on Liverot Street, she dreamed of doing great things for God. But the weeks turned into months and the months turned into years, without anything happening. It was as though God had forgotten her behind those cloistered walls.

Then one day Therese "turned to the letters of Saint Paul in hope of finally finding an answer." By chance her eyes fell upon Paul's First Letter to the Corinthians. At the end of the twelfth chapter, he explains that few people are called to be famous apostles or prophets. He then says, "I shall show you a still more excellent way" to holiness, that is, one that surpasses even these great callings. Then Paul launches into his celebrated essay on love.

After reading it, Therese wrote: "Nearly ecstatic with the supreme joy of my soul, I proclaimed: 'O Jesus, my love, at last I have found my calling: my call is love.' "

How deep is your hunger for holiness or righteousness? *Speak to Jesus about his own hunger for holiness.*

Day seven

"Blessed are the clean of heart,
for they will see God." Matthew 5:8

Seven-year-old Richard was the second youngest of nine children. Three days before Christmas, his mother asked him to shine her shoes for the holidays. After Richard was finished, he brought the shoes to his mother to see if they were all right. His mother was so delighted with his job that she gave him a quarter.

Later that day, when Richard's mother put on her shoes, her toe struck a hard lump. Removing the shoe, she found a quarter wrapped in paper. Written on the paper were these words: "Here's your quarter back, Mom. I shined your shoes out of love. [signed] Richard"

When Jesus said, "Blessed are the clean of heart," he was talking about people like Richard. He was talking about people whose motives are always unmixed. Their hearts are undivided. The person who is clean of heart is one who does things not to be seen by people or rewarded by them but for the eyes of God only. And for that reason, the person who is clean of heart will someday see God.

To what extent is your heart clean and undivided? What have you done that has not been rewarded? *Speak to Jesus about this.*

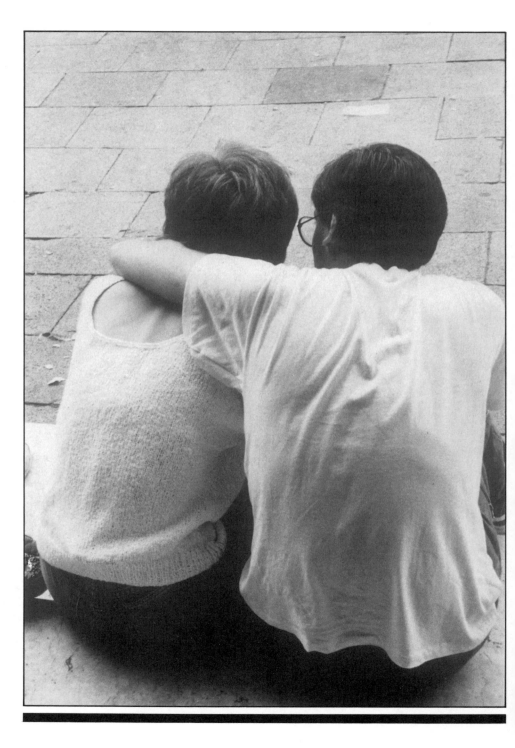

10
THE LOVING DISCIPLE

How ready are you
to love as Jesus loved?

"Love one another as I love you." John 15:12

In the movie *Shadow of the Hawk,* a young couple and an Indian guide are making their way up a mountainside. At one point the young woman slumps to the ground and says, "I can't take another step."

The young man lifts her to her feet and says, "But, darling, we must go on. We have no other choice." She shakes her head and says, "I can't do it." Then the Indian guide says to the young man, "Hold her close to your heart. Let your strength and courage and love flow out of your body into hers."

The young man does this, and in a few minutes the woman smiles and says, "Now I'm ready. I can go on."

We can all relate to that episode. There have been times in our lives when we, too, didn't think we could take another step. Then someone held us close to their heart and let their strength flow into us.

This week's meditations focus on love. The grace you ask for is this:

Lord, help me love others
as you love me.

During the week, you might wish to read the following New Testament passages about love:

The good Samaritan	Luke 10:25–37
The new commandment	John 15:9–17
Love for enemies	Luke 6:27–36
Primacy of love	1 Corinthians 13
God is love	1 John 4:7–21

As you read the passages, make them come alive again. For example, imagine you board a time machine and fly backward into time and are present as Jesus talks about love. Speak with Jesus after he finishes.

Or imagine you are the man Jesus talks about in the parable of the good Samaritan. Relive the man's experience of being attacked. Experience his surprise to find a Samaritan, whom Jews hated, taking care of him.

Or imagine you are present as Paul and John write their famous passages about love.

Our love should not be just words and talk;
it must be true love,
which shows itself in action.   1 John 3:18 (TEV)

"Metamorphosis" is a story about an unmarried man, named Gregor, who lives with his parents and sister. For years he's been a salesman, a slave to his boss and his customers. He smiles on the outside, but inside he's unhappy. He feels like an insect. Each night he dreams of his insectlike life. One morning he wakes up to discover that he's become what he feels like: a giant cockroach.

The tragedy is that the only way Gregor can become human again is if he is loved by humans, especially his family. But his appearance makes this impossible. The greater part of the story deals with Gregor's pathetic efforts to express himself to his family. In the end, he simply gives up and dies.

The story recalls another story, "The Beauty and the Beast," in which a witch turns a handsome prince into an ugly monster. The prince remains that way until a beautiful princess kisses him and changes him back into his handsome self again. In "Metamorphosis," the lovely princess never comes. Gregor remains a cockroach until he dies.

Who are the "Gregors" in today's world? *Speak to Jesus about specific things you are doing to reach out to these people.*

Day two

Love is patient, love is kind.   1 Corinthians 13:4

Alan Loy McGinnis tells this story about the author Dr. Norman Lobsenz.

Young Norman's wife was in the midst of a prolonged, serious illness. Norman was emotionally and physically drained. The ordeal was proving too much for him. One night he was on the verge of collapse. Suddenly an incident from his childhood flashed across his mind. It took place one night when his mother had taken seriously ill.

Norman had gotten up around midnight to get a drink of water. As he passed his parents' bedroom, he saw his father sitting in his bathrobe at the bedside of his mother. She was fast asleep. Norman rushed into the room and cried, "Daddy, is Mom worse?" "No, Norman," his father said quietly. "I'm just sitting here watching over her, in case she wakes up and needs something."

That long-forgotten incident from his childhood gave Norman all the strength he needed to carry on.

Recall a family episode from your childhood that is still a source of strength to you. *Speak to Jesus about your own initiative to anticipate the needs of others.*

Day three

*Love does not seek its own interests . . .
it does not brood over injury.*   1 Corinthians 13:5

Just before the 1986 Academy Awards, Barbara Walters interviewed President and Mrs. Reagan. One question she asked was how they had managed to keep their love alive across thirty-five years of married life.

When the Reagans didn't answer right away, Barbara tried to help, saying, "Was it because you were so willing to give and take on a 50–50 basis?"

The first lady broke into a gentle laugh and said, "Oh my, married life never breaks that evenly. Sometimes it's more like 90–10. So often one of us has had to give up so much more than the other."

That was a high point in the interview. It made a terribly important point: When it comes to love, you can't keep score. The day two people start to keep score, when it comes to love, is the day their love starts to die.

Married love—and all love—involves pain, sometimes lots of pain. And pain rarely divides itself evenly. More often it divides itself in a lopsided way.

How guilty are you of keeping score in friendships and love relationships? *Speak to Jesus about how he resisted the temptation to keep score in these areas.*

97

Day four

"Likewise a Levite . . . passed by." Luke 10:32

A woman was standing on a curb, waiting for the light to change. On the opposite curb was a girl of about seventeen. The woman noticed that the girl was crying.

When the light changed, each started across the street. Just as they were about to meet, the woman's motherly instincts came rushing to the surface. Every part of her wanted to reach out and comfort that girl. But the woman passed her by. She didn't even greet her. She just passed her by.

Hours later the tear-filled eyes of that girl continued to haunt the woman. Over and over she said to herself:

Why didn't I turn to that girl and say, "Honey, can I help?" Sure, she might have rejected me. But, so what! Only a few seconds would have been lost, but those few seconds would have been enough to let her know that someone cared. But instead, I passed on by. I acted as if she didn't exist.

Is there someone, right now, to whom you should be reaching out in love? *Speak to Jesus about how you can better translate your love into concrete action.*

Day five

Jesus was transfigured before them;
his face shone like the sun
and his clothes became white as light.
Matthew 17:2

England's television celebrity Malcolm Muggeridge went to India to film Mother Teresa and her sisters caring for the dying of Calcutta. The camera crew hadn't anticipated the poor lighting inside the building where the sisters worked, and didn't bring extra lights with them. They decided it was useless to film the sisters at work inside the building. But someone suggested they try anyway. Perhaps bits of the footage would be usable.

To everyone's surprise the footage was spectacular. It was illuminated by a mysterious light. Technically speaking, the camera crew says, the results were impossible to explain. Muggeridge has his own theory. He says:

Mother Teresa's Home for the Dying is overflowing with love. . . . [One] senses [this] immediately on entering it. This love is luminous, like the haloes that artists have seen and made visible round the heads of saints. I find it not at all surprising that the luminosity should register on photographic film.

Recall a time when another person radiated God's love to you at a time when you needed it. *Speak to Jesus about his own efforts to radiate love to an unloving world.*

Day six

Jesus wept. So the Jews said,
"See how much he loved Lazarus." John 11:35–36

Years ago the actor Jimmy Stewart wrote an article for *McCall's*. In it he described an incident that took place just before his bomber squadron went overseas during World War II.

As the moment of departure neared, Jimmy sensed that his father wanted to say something special to him. But the words never came out. Finally his dad hugged him and departed. Only later did Jimmy discover that his father had slipped a letter into his pocket. It read:

Soon after you read this letter, you will be on your way to the worst sort of danger. . . . I am banking on the enclosed copy of the 91st Psalm. The thing that takes the place of fear . . . is the promise of these words. . . . I love you more than I can tell you. [signed] Dad

Jimmy was struck especially by these words: "Under God's wings you shall take refuge. . . . To his angels God has given command about you, that they guard you in all your ways." *Psalm 91:4, 11*

How hard is it for you to express love in an external way to others? Recall some recent times when you had trouble expressing your love. *Speak to Jesus about his own external expressions of love.*

> *I have been put to death with Christ
> on his cross,
> so that it is no longer I who live,
> but it is Christ who lives in me.*
> Galatians 2:19–20 (TEV)

The musical *Man of La Mancha* was inspired by the life and work of the Spanish writer Cervantes. Born in cruel poverty, he became a soldier and was captured in battle. He was sentenced to years of slavery in Africa. Broken in body, he died in 1616, after completing his major work, *Don Quixote.*

Near the end of the musical, Quixote is dying. At his side is Aldonza, a worthless woman whom he idealized and called Dulcinea. Quixote loved her with a pure love, unlike anything she had previously experienced.

When Quixote dies, Aldonza sings "The Impossible Dream." At the end of the song someone shouts, "Aldonza." She replies, "My name is now Dulcinea." Thanks to Quixote's love, the worthless Aldonza had died, and in her place was born Quixote's Dulcinea. Pure love had changed a worthless wretch into a beautiful human being.

How is the Quixote story a parable of Jesus and you? *Speak to Jesus about the impact your own love can have on the world in which you walk and work.*

11
THE FORGIVING DISCIPLE

How ready are you to forgive as Jesus forgave?

Be kind . . . forgiving one another
as God has forgiven you in Christ.   Ephesians 4:32

Richard Pindell wrote a short story called "Somebody's Son."

It opens with a runaway boy named David, who is writing a letter home to his mother. He expresses the hope that his old-fashioned father will forgive him and accept him again as a son. The boy writes:

In a few days I'll be passing our property. If Dad'll take me back, ask him to tie a white cloth on the apple tree in the field next to our house.

Days later David is seated on a train, which is rapidly approaching his house. Soon the tree will be visible around the next bend. But David can't bring himself to look at it. He's afraid the white cloth won't be there. Turning to the man sitting next to him, he says, nervously, "Mister, will you do me a favor?

Around the bend on the right, you'll see a tree. Tell me if there's a white cloth tied to it."

As the train rumbles past the tree, David stares straight ahead. Then in a quaking voice he asks the man, "Mister, is a white cloth tied to one of the branches of the tree?" The man answers in a surprised voice, "Why, son, there's a white cloth tied to practically every branch!"

That story is a parable of God's forgiveness of us. As God forgives us, so Jesus asks us to forgive one another. This week's meditations focus on the readiness to forgive. The grace you ask for is this:

Lord, help me forgive others
as you forgive me.

During the week, you might wish to read the following passages on forgiveness. As you do, make them come alive in your imagination.

The town sinner	Luke 7:36–50
The lost sheep	Luke 15:1–7
The lost coin	Luke 15:8–10
The lost son	Luke 15:11–32
The unforgiving man	Matthew 18:21–35
The adulteress	John 8:1–11

Day one

"Lord, if my brother sins against me,
how often must I forgive him?
As many as seven times?"
Jesus answered, "I say to you,
not seven times but seventy-seven times."
Matthew 18:21-22

The singing career of Grammy award winner Marvin Gaye ended in tragedy on April 1, 1983. He was shot to death by his own father.

A year later David Ritz, Gaye's close friend, wrote Gaye's biography. He entitled it *Divided Soul.*

Gaye was indeed a divided soul. He was part artist and part entertainer, part sinner and part saint, part macho man and part gentleman.

Gaye's childhood was tormented by cruelty inflicted upon him by his father. It left a wound that never healed. Commenting on this, Ritz says of his friend:

He really believed in Jesus a lot, but he could never apply the teaching of Jesus on forgiveness to his own father. In the end it destroyed them both.

Name one person from whom are you withholding full love. *Speak to Jesus about this situation, and ask him to help you deal with it in a more loving way.*

Day two

"Ask and you will receive." Luke 11:9

Corrie ten Boom and her family were imprisoned by the Nazis during World War II for hiding Jews in Amsterdam. Only Corrie survived the terrible prison ordeal.

When the war ended, Corrie traveled about Europe, lecturing on forgiveness and reconciliation. After a talk in Munich, Germany, a man came up to thank her for the talk. He was one of the hated prison guards.

When the man reached out to shake her hand, Corrie froze. She couldn't believe her response. She had just given a talk on forgiveness, and now she herself couldn't forgive the man.

Corrie began to pray, saying, "Jesus, I cannot forgive this man. Help me forgive him."

At that moment some mysterious power helped her reach out and take the man's hand in true forgiveness.

That episode taught Corrie a great truth. The same Jesus who gives the command to forgive also gives us the grace to obey the command. All we need do is ask for it.

How hard is it for you to forgive from the heart? Recall some times when it was difficult for you to forgive. *Speak to Jesus about his ability to do this, especially while hanging in pain on the cross.*

Day three

Do not look for revenge. . . .
Do not be conquered by evil
but conquer evil with good.   Romans 12:19, 21

Marcia Hootman and Patt Perkins wrote a book entitled *How to Forgive Your Ex-Husband.* It describes extensive research on the anger of women going through divorce. From the research the authors draw two disturbing conclusions.

First, an appalling amount of energy and money is wasted by women trying to get even with their ex-husbands.

Second, many of these women are now hurting *themselves* more by their anger than they were hurt by their former spouses.

Explaining their reason for writing the book, the authors say that they "just want women to get rid of the anger," which is "so destructive," and to get on with their lives.

The authors go on to say that forgiveness does not mean forgoing justice. They cite Pope John Paul II as an example of this. After he was shot, he went to the prison to forgive his assailant, Mehmet Ali Agca. "But you notice," they say, "the pope did not ask that Agca be let out on parole."

Are you holding any grudges now? In the film *The Karate Kid,* Mr. Miyagi warns Daniel, "Who pursues revenge should dig two graves." *Speak to Jesus about Miyagi's point and its importance.*

Day four

> *"Do good to those who hate you,*
> *bless those who curse you."* Luke 6:27-28

Father Paul Belliveau is a missionary from Flushing, New York. His parish is a refugee camp in Honduras. It houses over ten thousand Salvadoran refugees. The Salvadoran army surrounds the camp, holding them prisoner.

One Sunday Father Belliveau gave his homily on the language of hate, which consists of three key words: *accuse, condemn,* and *eliminate.* He noted that both the guerrillas and the Salvadoran army use this language in their radio programs.

Father Paul concluded, saying, "Jesus refuses to play this game. He uses the language of love, which forgives in a world of hate." Many people got upset.

After Mass a young man grabbed the microphone and shouted, "Father Paul said we all have to love and forgive, but that's easy to say." Another man shouted into the mike, "Father Paul doesn't understand our situation."

What would you have said to the people if someone had handed you the mike? *Speak to Jesus about why he refused to play the game of hate when he walked our earth.*

"Pray for those who mistreat you."   Luke 6:28

Mrs. Hannah is a widow in Colorado. One day her daughter was murdered. The assailant was captured, found guilty, and imprisoned. But Mrs. Hannah could not forgive him. She knew that Jesus said, "Pray for those who mistreat you," but she couldn't do it.

Worse yet, Mrs. Hannah felt the love that once characterized her personality fading from her life. She felt herself being destroyed by her own hatred and anger. She didn't know what to do or where to turn.

Then one day, after thinking about Jesus' teaching, Mrs. Hannah decided to act on it, in spite of her feelings. She bought a Bible, wrote a note of forgiveness in it, and sent it to the prisoner.

The prisoner, who had become withdrawn and bitter, couldn't believe what Mrs. Hannah had done. He sent word to her that she had opened the door to a new world for him. Before receiving her note, he had all but despaired of God's forgiveness. After receiving it, he realized that if she could forgive him, so could God.

———————

Relive Mrs. Hannah's anger after the death of her daughter. Relive her joy after forgiving the prisoner and reading his note. *Speak to Jesus about the power of forgiveness.*

Day six

In your light we see light.   Psalm 36:10

In the novel *All Quiet on the Western Front,* a young German soldier lies in a shell crater taking cover from artillery fire. Suddenly a French soldier leaps into the same hole, seeking cover also. The young German bayonets him.

As the French soldier dies slowly, the young German is moved to pity for him. He gives him a drink from his own canteen. Then the Frenchman dies.

This is the first man the German has killed, and he wonders what the Frenchman's name is. Seeing a wallet in the dead man's pocket, he takes it out. In it is a photograph of a young mother holding a little girl. The German youth gets a lump in his throat. The dead man is not an enemy but a father and a husband, a man like himself, who loves and is loved. Touched deeply, he copies the dead man's address. He will write a letter to his wife.

What happened in the shell hole? Did the German suddenly realize his Christian duty to love his enemy, and force himself to love the dying soldier? Not at all. He simply saw his enemy in a whole new light. And this changed vision gave him a changed attitude.

Relive the German's feelings as he looked at the photograph. *Ask Jesus to help you see your enemies as he sees them and loves them.*

*Therefore, I urge you
to reaffirm your love for him.*   2 Corinthians 2:8

John Catoir cites this incident in his book *That Your Joy May Be Full.*

A widow wrote to Ann Landers. She didn't want advice. She just wanted to thank Ann for the advice she had given someone else eight years before. It had helped her too.

The advice was to the mother of several small children. Her husband had done something stupid, and Ann urged the young mother to forgive and forget. "Don't be stupid or proud," she said. "Take him back. I promise you won't regret it."

The widow said she was in the same situation herself at the time. She didn't see how she could forgive and forget, but she decided that since Ann advised it, she'd try.

What happened? The widow told Ann that the years that followed were the happiest of their whole married life. "The warmth of the memories of our last years together," she wrote, "will sustain me forever."

Recall a time when you were truly forgiving. *Speak to Jesus about why he was so able to forgive and forget.*

12
THE PRAYING DISCIPLE

How ready are you to pray as Jesus prayed?

Jesus would withdraw to deserted places to pray. Luke 5:16

Irmgard Wood lived in Stuttgart, Germany, during World War II. One morning her mother and sisters saw an American plane catch fire and fall from the sky. Instinctively, they prayed for the pilot, even though he was an American.

Years later the Wood family migrated to the United States. Irmgard's mother got a job in a hospital in the San Fernando Valley in California. One day a patient detected her German accent and asked her whereabouts she lived in Germany. "Stuttgart," she replied.

"Stuttgart!"said the patient. "I almost got killed in Stuttgart. One morning during World War II, my plane caught fire and fell from the sky. Somebody must have really been praying for me that day."

That story recalls the words of the British poet Alfred Lord Tennyson: "More things are wrought through prayer than this world dreams of."

This week's meditations focus on prayer. The grace you ask for is this:

Lord, help me pray as you prayed.

During the week you may feel inspired to read about Jesus and prayer. Here are some passages you will find helpful.

Prayer instruction	Luke 11:1–13
Persevering in prayer	Luke 18:1–8
Two pray-ers	Luke 18:9–14
Hilltop prayer	Luke 9:26–36
Lord's Prayer	Matthew 6:7–13
Last Supper prayer	John 17:1–26
Gethsemane prayer	Matthew 26:36–46

"Ask and you will receive."   Luke 11:9

A student, named Bill, was turning his young teacher, Mary, into a nervous wreck. One morning before school Mary was at her desk writing something in shorthand. Bill appeared.

"Whatdaya writing?" he said. "It's a prayer to God," she replied. "Can God read shorthand?" Bill joked. "He can do anything, even answer this prayer," Mary said, slipping the note inside her Bible. Then she turned to write on the board. As she did, Bill stole the note and slipped it into his book.

Twenty years later Bill was going through a box of boyhood belongings. He came across the book—and the note, which was now faded with age. He stared at it, wondering what it said. Then he put it in his wallet.

Back at the office, he asked his secretary to translate it. It read: "Dear God, I can't handle my class with Bill upsetting it. Touch his heart. He's someone who can become very good or very evil."

Weeks later Bill tracked down his old teacher to thank her for that prayer. It had been answered beyond her wildest dreams.

Relive the feelings Mary had when she learned how her prayer had been answered. Who might you pray for, right now, as she prayed for Bill? *Speak to Jesus about the power of prayer.*

_____
_____
_____
_____
_____

Day two

"All that you ask for in prayer,
believe that you will receive it
and it shall be yours."   Mark 11:24

Jim Johnson's job was to save a failing hotel. It was a desperate situation. Jim decided to do something radical. Each night he drove to a hill overlooking the hotel. He parked and sat there for twenty minutes—praying.

Jim prayed for the hotel guests, behind the lighted windows. He prayed for the hotel employees and their families. He prayed for the people who did business with the hotel.

Gradually, things began to happen at the hotel. A new confidence radiated from its employees. A new warmth welcomed each new guest. A new spirit permeated the hotel's operation. Within a year the hotel experienced a remarkable rebirth.

Norman Vincent Peale, who tells the story, credits the hotel's rebirth to the nightly prayer of Jim Johnson.

Peale ends his story with a fascinating thought: If the prayer of one man could transform a hotel, think how the prayer of a nation could transform the world.

What is your reaction to Peale's thought? How trusting are you in Jesus' promises about prayer? *Speak to Jesus about why he prayed.*

116

Day three

Pray without ceasing.   2 Thessalonians 5:17

"Prayer is one of the ways that God chose to share his infinite power with us," said Blaise Pascal, the French mathematician. His point is this. Just as God shares his power with us by making us "thinking" persons, so God shares his power with us by making us "praying" persons.

It's noteworthy that not everyone can impact human affairs greatly by thought. But everyone—even someone with a low I.Q.—can do so by prayer.

The great God of heaven and earth created us to be more than mere spectators of his creative power. God created us to be sharers in it. This is part of what it means to be made in the "image and likeness" of God.

Alexis Carrel, the Nobel prize surgeon, summed up the power of prayer this way:

Prayer is the most powerful form of energy one can generate. The influence of prayer on the human mind and body is as demonstrable as that of secreting glands. Prayer is a force as real as terrestrial gravity.

Do you really believe that neglecting God's gift of prayer is as serious as neglecting his gift of intelligence? *Speak to God about your biggest problem when it comes to prayer.*

117

Day four

After . . . kneeling, Jesus prayed.   Luke 22:41

In Washington, D.C., there's a striking statue of Abraham Lincoln at prayer. It's the work of artist Spencer Houk.

Houk got his inspiration for the statue from a story that his grandfather told over and over. One day he was walking through a woods in Gettysburg. Suddenly he came upon a kneeling figure. It was President Lincoln.

General Sickles recalls a similar episode. Shortly before the Battle of Gettysburg, President Lincoln felt crushed by the weight of responsibility on his shoulders. Instinctively, he turned to God in prayer. Commenting on that prayer, Lincoln himself said:

Never before had I prayed with such earnestness. I wish I could repeat my prayer. I felt that I must put all my trust in Almighty God. . . . He alone could save the nation from destruction.

When Lincoln rose from his knees, he said, "I felt my prayer was answered. . . . I had no misgiving about the result."

Recall one of the most fervent prayers you ever made. *Speak to Jesus about your failure to pray as faithfully and trustingly as he prayed.*

Day five

*Jesus would withdraw to deserted places
to pray.* Luke 5:16

Adelaide Proctor's poem "A Legend" tells about a monk whose preaching attracted crowds and changed people's lives. Every time he preached, an old man sat nearby and prayed.

One day the monk was thanking God for his power to move hearts, when an angel said something to this effect: "My son, it isn't your preaching that lights up people's hearts and changes them. It's the old man's praying."

In other words, the monk's preaching was needed, but it wasn't the important thing. The important thing was the old man's praying.

We might compare the monk's preaching to the cord of a lamp, and the old man's prayers to the current flowing through the cord. The cord doesn't cause the lamp to light up; it's the current flowing through the cord.

The point is this. What our world needs in order to get people to change their lives is not more preaching but more praying. We've got plenty of preachers but far too few "pray-ers."

Have you ever prayed that the Sunday homilist's words would touch people's hearts—including your own? *Speak to Jesus about the advisability of doing this on a regular basis.*

119

Day six

Jesus raised his eyes to heaven. John 17:1

In *The Inner Game of Tennis,* W. Timothy Galwey points out that when we watch a game of tennis, we see only the *outer* game: what happens on the court. We don't see the *inner* game: what happens in the players' minds.

What is true of tennis is true of prayer. Prayer has an outer dimension and an inner dimension. The Gospels tell us about both dimensions of Jesus' prayer.

Outwardly, Jesus prayed in various ways: kneeling (Luke 22:41), face downward (Matthew 26:39). He also prayed with eyes raised to heaven (Mark 7:34), out loud (Matthew 26:42), and with perseverance (Matthew 26:44–45).

Inwardly, Jesus also prayed in various ways: *free* prayers and *fixed* prayers. His free prayers came spontaneously from his heart in his own words. For example, he prayed that way at the Last Supper (John 17:1). Jesus also prayed fixed prayers; that is, he used memorized prayers that had been part of the Jewish faith for centuries. For example, on the cross Jesus prayed Psalm 22 (Mark 15:34).

How important do you consider your body to be to your prayer? How important do you consider memorized prayer to be? *Speak to Jesus about what motivated him to pray.*

Day seven

"This is how you are to pray:
'Our Father . . . ' "   Matthew 6:9

Two things stand out in the Our Father (Lord's Prayer): the word *Father* and the structure of the prayer.

First, the word for "father" which Jesus used was *Abba,* a title of affection, like our word *daddy.* In other words, Jesus taught us to address God with the affection and trust of a small child addressing its father.

Second, the structure of the Lord's Prayer divides into two sets of requests:

1. Three "your" petitions—"Hallowed be *your* name, *your* kingdom come, *your* will be done"
2. Three "our" petitions—"give us today *our* daily bread," "forgive us *our* debts," "deliver *us* from the evil one"

The "your" petitions look to God; the "our" petitions look to ourselves. That is the proper order for all true prayer. First we turn to God. Then we turn to our needs.

The "our" petitions embrace all times—and all needs: the *present* ("give us today our daily bread"), the *past* ("forgive us our debts"), and the *future* ("deliver us from the evil one").

Pray the Lord's Prayer slowly and in a low voice, pausing briefly to reflect on each petition. *Speak to Jesus about why he taught us this prayer.*

13
THE SERVING DISCIPLE

How ready are you to serve as Jesus served?

"Whoever wishes to be great among you will be your servant." Mark 10:43

Dr. Elisabeth Kubler-Ross is a former professor of psychiatry at the University of Chicago. She wrote a best-seller called *Death and Dying.* The book grew out of interviews with hundreds of people who had been declared clinically dead and then revived.

Repeatedly these people report that during their experience they underwent a kind of instant replay of their lives. It was like seeing a movie of everything they'd ever done.

How did the instant replay affect these people? Did it reveal anything significant? Commenting on this, Dr. Kubler-Ross says:

When you come to this point, you see there are only two things that are relevant: the service you rendered to others and love. All those things we think are important, like fame, money, prestige, and power, are insignificant.

This week's meditations focus on loving service of others. The grace you ask for is this:

Lord, help me serve others lovingly
as you did.

During the week, you may feel moved to read some of the things the Bible says about loving service. A few passages to read and ponder are these:

What does God want?	Isaiah 58:5–12
Who is the greatest?	Mark 10:35–45
Wash one another's feet.	John 13:1–17
A reversal of fortunes	Luke 16:19–31
When were you hungry?	Matthew 25:31–46

Day one

"I was hungry and you gave me food."
Matthew 25:35

An old monk prayed many years for a vision from God. One day it came. But then, right in the middle of the vision, the monastery bell rang. It was time to feed the poor who gathered daily at the monastery gate.

It was the old monk's turn to feed them. If he failed to show up with food, the unfortunate people would leave quietly, thinking the monastery had nothing to give them that day.

The old monk was torn between his earthly duty and his heavenly vision. But before the bell stopped ringing, the monk made his decision. With a heavy heart, he turned his back on the vision and went off to feed the poor.

Nearly an hour later, the old monk returned to his room. When he opened the door, he could hardly believe his eyes. There in the room was the vision, waiting for him.

As the monk dropped to his knees in thanksgiving, the vision said to him, "My son, had you not gone off to feed the poor, I would not have stayed."

How does the point of this story apply to your life? *Speak to Jesus about your own concrete involvement in feeding the hungry.*

Day two

Eddie Fischer knew what questions television reporters would ask when they showed up with their cameras: "Why are you walking from Guatemala to Pennsylvania?"

I'm trying to raise money for a water system for Rabinal, Guatemala. The thirty thousand Indians living there have been without uncontaminated drinking water since the earthquake.

"How did a twenty-one-year-old American kid get involved with a Guatemalan town?"

I went there as a volunteer to help the people rebuild. A water system costs $300,000, and they didn't have that kind of money. So when it came time for me to return home, I decided I'd try to raise the money by walking home.

Eddie reached home six months and four thousand miles later. His "Walk for Water" netted $300,000—right on target.

What keeps you from volunteering your time to help people less fortunate than you. *Speak to Jesus about why so few people—including yourself—are ready to do the kind of thing Eddie Fischer did.*

Day three

*"I was . . . a stranger
and you welcomed me."* Matthew 25:35

An old man collapsed on a downtown Brooklyn street corner. An ambulance rushed him to Kings County Hospital.

From a blurred envelope in the man's wallet, nurses deciphered the name and address of a marine, who appeared to be his son. They put through an emergency call to North Carolina, where the son was stationed.

When the marine arrived, the nurse said to the old man inside the oxygen tent, "Your son's here." With that, the man, who was heavily sedated, reached out his hand feebly. The marine took it and held it tenderly for the next four hours.

Occasionally the nurse suggested that the young man take a break and walk around for a while. But he refused.

About dawn the old man died. After he passed away, the marine said to the nurse, "Who was that man?" The nurse said, "Wasn't that your father?" "No," said the marine, "but I saw he needed a son, so I stayed."

Relive the marine's experience as he ministered to the old man. *Speak to Jesus about his own ministry to others and how you might begin to imitate it.*

Day four

"I was . . . naked and you clothed me."
Matthew 25:35-36

Sister Emmanuelle lives and works among the ten thousand garbage pickers of Cairo. These "poorest of the poor" survive by scouring the city's garbage dump.

Sister's day begins at four-thirty as she wakes in a hut with a hole in the roof. After washing in a bucket of water, she walks two miles to attend Mass. That walk takes her past piles of rotting garbage and packs of snarling dogs.

At nine o'clock she begins teaching Arabic to about forty children. She ends by reading from the Bible and teaching them how to pray. Then she visits families, writing down their pressing needs in a notebook. Sister Emmanuelle is a gentle person, says *Time* magazine. But "her gentleness turns to steel when she browbeats the bureaucrats and the bankers to help her garbage pickers."

Time ends its story by calling Sister Emmanuelle the best of the "new missionaries." They quote her as saying that she plans to continue to serve her garbage pickers until the day she dies.

How willing would you be to take a year off of your life—if this were feasible for you—to help someone like Sister Emmanuelle? *Speak to Jesus about the pros and cons of doing this.*

128

Day five

"I was . . . ill and you cared for me."
Matthew 25:35–36

An old native in New Guinea used to read the Gospel to outpatients while they waited to be treated at the missionary clinic. One day he experienced trouble reading. The doctor checked his eyes and found that the man was rapidly going blind.

The next day the old man didn't show up to read. Someone said he had gone off to the hills alone.

A week later a boy led the doctor to the old man's hideout. "What are you doing here?" said the doctor. "Why didn't you stay at the hospital?" The old man replied that ever since he learned that he was going blind, he had spent all of his time memorizing stories and passages from the Bible. He said:

You ask the boy. He has been listening to me as I repeat from memory what I've learned. The last few days I've been repeating and repeating to make sure I've got it correctly. Soon I'm coming back to the hospital, Doctor, to tell the outpatients about Jesus.

Why are you reluctant to share your faith with others as enthusiastically as the old man did? *Speak to Jesus about what motivated him to share his faith with everyone.*

129

Day six

*"I was . . . in prison
and you visited me."* Matthew 25:35–36

Saint Peter Claver was a Jesuit priest who worked among the black slaves in South America in the seventeenth century. Here is an excerpt from one of his letters:

Yesterday . . . feast of the Holy Trinity, a great number of black people who had been seized along the African rivers were put ashore from one very large vessel. We hurried out with two baskets full of oranges, lemons, sweet biscuits and all sorts of things. . . . There was a number of them lying on damp earth, or rather mud. . . . They were naked without any covering at all.

We took off our cloaks, went to a store, brought from there all the wood available and put it together to make a platform; then forcing a way through the guards, we eventually managed to carry all the sick to it. . . . You should have seen the expression of gratitude in their eyes! In this way we spoke to them, not with words but with deeds. Any other form of address would have been pointless.

Imagine you are a slave lying in the mud, naked and sick. *Relive the slave's experience, and talk to God about it.*

130

Day seven

"Whatever you did
for one of these least brothers of mine,
you did for me." Matthew 25:40

Eighty-one-year-old Lorraine Hale has helped nearly six hundred babies withdraw from drugs over the past sixteen years. These tiny victims were born to junkie mothers and became addicted in the womb. They shake, vomit, suffer from a runny nose and bad diarrhea. It usually takes four to six weeks for them to withdraw.

Mother Hale began this work in her own house in Harlem, using her own money. Sometimes she was caring for twenty babies at one time in her crowded home. She says:

They reach out to you in pain and cry, and all you can do is hold them and love them. Drug babies are like any other babies; they just need a lot of love.

Mother Hale's work went largely unnoticed until President Reagan heard about it. Since then enough money has come in to allow Mother Hale's work to expand to include a staff and a fully equipped center.

Relive the way Mother Hale felt one day when she learned that she had almost exhausted her personal funds helping these babies. *Talk to Jesus about the faith that kept her going.*

14
DECISION

How can you follow Jesus more closely?

"Follow me."   Mark 2:14

A fifteen-year-old boy and his father were driving past a tiny airport in Ohio. A low-flying plane suddenly spun out of control and nose-dived into the runway. The boy yelled, "Dad! Dad! Stop the car!" Moments later the boy was pulling the pilot out of the plane. He was a twenty-year-old student flier, who was practicing takeoffs and landings. The young man died in the boy's arms.

When the boy arrived home, he threw his arms around his mother and cried, "Mom, he was my friend! He was only twenty!" That night the boy was too shocked to eat supper. He went to his room, closed the door, and lay on his bed.

The boy was working part-time in a drugstore. Every penny he made he spent on flying lessons. His goal was to get his pilot's license when he turned sixteen.

The boy's parents wondered what effect the tragedy would have on their son. Would he stop taking lessons, or would he continue? They agreed that the decision must be his.

Two days later the boy's mother brought some freshly baked cookies to her son's room. On his dresser she saw an open notebook. It was the one he had kept from childhood. Across the top of the page was written, in big letters, "The Character of Jesus." Beneath was listed a series of qualities:

Jesus was sinless;
he was humble;
he championed the poor;
he was unselfish;
he was close to God . . .

The mother saw that in her son's hour of decision he was turning to Jesus for guidance. Then she turned to her son and said, "What have you decided about flying?" The boy looked at her and said, "Mom, I hope you and Dad will understand, but with God's help, I must continue to fly."

That boy was Neil Armstrong. And on July 20, 1969, he became the first human being to walk on the moon. Few people who watched that historic event on television knew that one of the reasons Neil Armstrong was walking on the moon was Jesus. They didn't know that it was from Jesus that he drew strength and guidance to make a crucial teenage decision about flying.

Consider a second story. In January 1973, Joe Paterno, head coach at Penn State, was offered $1 million to coach the New England Patriots. He was thrilled by the offer and phoned Patriot owner Billy Sullivan that he would meet with him in New York the following morning.

That night Joe Paterno could not sleep. The next morning, after deep reflection, Paterno phoned Sullivan and turned down the $1-million offer. Later he explained his decision to sports writers. He said the opportunity to impact the lives of college students

134

was more important than the money and prestige he would get from being a pro coach.

Both of these stories involve important decisions. Both involve trying to discern God's will about the decisions.

This week's meditations focus on discerning God's will about a decision you may wish to make. The grace you ask for is this:

Lord, help me know and do your will.

This raises a question. How do you discern God's will about a decision? For example, how do you seek God's will about your life's calling, as Armstrong did? How do you decide on whether to make a change in your life's work, as Paterno did?

In his *Spiritual Exercises,* Saint Ignatius says there are three times when crucial decisions can be made.

The first time is when you are absolutely clear about what to do. Think of Saint Paul on the road to Damascus (Acts 9:1-15). There was no doubt in his mind about what God wanted him to do.

The second time is when you experience agitation about what to do. Think of Joe Paterno being pulled one way, then the other. In times like this, you can "test" the pulls to see which is from God. Paterno rightly concluded that the one that brought him inner peace was the right one.

The third decision time is when you experience neither clarity nor agitation. Think of Neil Armstrong. He felt no great pull either way after the plane crash. He simply wanted to reevaluate his decision about making flying his future career. After weighing the pros and cons and praying, he decided to continue flying. When it comes to this third decision time, Saint Ignatius recommends two procedures for discerning God's will. The first involves six steps.

1. Clarify the decision you must make and the choices that are open to you.

135

2. Recall that your decision should accord with God's purpose in creating you: to share your life and your love with him and with other people forever.

3. Pray for the grace to be open to the right choice.

4. List reasons for and against each choice.

5. Determine which choice seems to be more in keeping with God's purpose in creating you.

6. Make your decision, asking God to confirm that it is the right one.

The second procedure involves five steps.

1. Ask yourself, "Are the pulls I feel for or against any of the choices based on worldly or selfish motives or on love for God?"

2. Imagine you are a person you have never met before. You take a liking to this person and want the best for him or her. Ask yourself, "What would I counsel that person to do if he or she had to make the same decision I do?"

3. Imagine yourself at the moment of death. Ask yourself, "Which choice will likely give me the greatest joy at that time?"

4. Imagine yourself before the judgment seat of God after your death. Ask yourself, "Which choice will likely give me the greatest joy at that moment?"

5. Make your decision, asking God to confirm it as being the right one.

One final observation about decisions. Often you are not faced with a decision about your life's calling or a change or modification within that calling. Rather (at least with adults), it's a decision about how you are living out a choice already made, perhaps years ago.

Your task, therefore, is to evaluate how well you are living out that choice. Are you doing it in a way that is in keeping with God's purpose in creating you? Are you doing it in a way that will bring you the greatest joy when you render an account of your life to God after your death?

Day one

*"Things that cause sin
will inevitably occur,
but woe to the person
through whom they occur."* Luke 17:1

Bubba Smith, former college and pro football star, is also famous for his beer commercials.

In October 1985, Michigan State honored Bubba by making him the grand marshal of their homecoming parade. Bubba was thrilled to be back at his alma mater. As he rode through the student-lined streets, one side started shouting, "Tastes great." The other side shouted back, "Less filling." It was obvious that Bubba's beer commercials were a hit.

That night Bubba was deeply disturbed by the number of students at the parade who were "drunk out of their heads." Then and there he made a decision to stop making the commercials. He feared that they were influencing young people to do something he didn't want to be a part of. The decision cost Bubba a lot of money, but he thought something much greater was at stake.

Recall a decision that cost you a great deal to make. *Speak to Jesus about his ability and courage to make the right decision, regardless of personal cost.*

137

Day two

"You will be led before governors and kings for my sake." Matthew 10:18

The South Korean poet Kim Chi Ha was sentenced to life in prison for writing poems critical of the South Korean dictatorship. The poems condemned the government's treatment of Korea's poor and rejected. In 1976 the government added a further seven years to his life sentence. After the ruling, Kim Chi Ha said to his mother, jokingly, "I must stay in prison seven years after I die."

Kim Chi Ha's mother backs her son. She agrees with him when he says of Christians:

"We must be for the poor and oppressed of society. Society puts these people down, but the gospel tells us they are important. There is a real struggle against evil in the world, and we must take this world seriously."

Kim Chi Ha's mother concludes:

I want to follow my son's statement. . . . I want to identify with the oppressed, the troubled, the despised. . . . This is my dream, my faith. Maryknoll magazine

How seriously do you take the struggle against evil in our world? *Speak to Jesus about what motivated him to keep struggling against evil, even when the struggle seemed futile.*

138

Day three

*"My child, remember that you received
what was good during your lifetime
while Lazarus . . . received
what was bad."* Luke 16:25

At the age of thirty, Albert Schweitzer gave up
a brilliant career in music, studied medicine, and
became a missionary doctor in Africa.

One gospel story that played a big role in his
decision was the parable of Lazarus and the rich
man. It describes a rich man who feasted daily at an
overflowing table. Lazarus, on the other hand, lay at
the gates of the rich man's house, begging for food.
But the rich man ignored him, feasting his dogs
instead.

Eventually both Lazarus and the rich man died.
In the next world their plights were reversed. It was
only then that the rich man realized how callous and
cruel he had been.

When Schweitzer read the parable, he reasoned
that his African brother was Lazarus and that he was
the rich man. Then he asked himself, "How can I
indulge myself in pleasure, while my African brother
endures pain?"

How would you answer Schweitzer's question?
Speak to Jesus about your answer.

Day four

*"The harvest is abundant
but the laborers are few."* Luke 10:2

In the years following the discovery of America, Francis Xavier was a high jumper at the University of Paris.

One day he was deeply moved by Jesus' words, "What profit is there for one to gain the whole world yet lose or forfeit himself?" *Luke 9:25* The more Francis thought about those words, the more he was moved by them. Eventually he turned his back on the glamour and excitement of university life and became a missionary to India. In a letter to some close friends, he wrote:

Many out here fail to become Christians only because there is nobody prepared to undertake the task of teaching them about Christ. I have often felt moved to go to the universities of Europe, especially to the Sorbonne in Paris, shouting like a madman, saying to those who have more learning than goodwill, to employ it advantageously. If only, while they studied their humanities, they would also study the accounting that God will ask for the talent he has given them!

How seriously have you ever considered turning your back on the world and doing what Francis did? *Speak to Jesus about your future.*

_____

_____

_____

_____

_____

_____

_____

Day five

*Teach me, LORD . . . to serve you
with complete devotion.*   Psalm 86:11 (TEV)

When Charlie DeLeo returned from Vietnam, he got a job as a maintenance worker at the Statue of Liberty. Among other things, he had to keep the two hundred glass windows in the crown and torch clean and make sure their sodium vapor lights were always working.

Pointing to the torch, Charlie says proudly, "That's my chapel. I dedicated it to the Lord, and I go up there on my breaks and meditate." One day Charlie wrote this prayer:

*O Lord,
I don't ever expect to have
the faith of Abraham . . .
nor the strength of Samson,
nor the courage of David . . .
nor the wisdom of Solomon. . . .
But what I do expect, O Lord,
is your calling on me some day.
What is your will, I shall do,
what is your command shall be my joy. . . .
And I shall not fail you, O Lord,
for you are all I seek to serve.*
(slightly paraphrased)

Repeat Charlie's prayer slowly, pausing to let each thought sink in. Then repeat the prayer phrase by phrase in a loud whisper. *Listen with the ear of your soul to God's reply to you.*

Day six

He himself bore our sins in his body. . . .
By his wounds you have been healed.
1 Peter 2:24

The novel *Great Expectations* concerns a boy named Pip, who comes from a poor, lower-class family. One day Pip is kind to a stranger, whom everyone else rejects.

Months later a lawyer shows up at Pip's home, saying that Pip is to receive a large sum of money, annually, from an anonymous donor. There is one stipulation. Pip is to be sent to London, educated in the best schools, and brought up as a "gentleman." Pip's life changes beyond his wildest dreams.

Years later a crude, lower-class man shows up at Pip's beautiful London home. Pip is rude to him and tries to run him off.

Then comes the surprise. The man turns out to be the stranger Pip befriended years before. He is also the anonymous donor of the money. He has dedicated his life to hard work to give Pip a new life.

When the man takes Pip's clean, smooth hands into his dirty, rough hands and kisses them, Pip is too repentant and stunned to speak.

How is this story a kind of parable of Jesus and you? If Jesus has done so much for you, what are you willing to do for him? *Speak to Jesus about this.*

Day seven

I have set before you life and death. . . .
Choose life.   Deuteronomy 30:19

There is a tide in the affairs of men
Which, taken at the flood, leads on to fortune;
Omitted, all the voyage of life
Is bound in shallows and in miseries.
William Shakespeare, *Julius Caesar*

Shakespeare's point is that there comes a time in life when you must take your destiny into your own hands and decide your future. You are face-to-face with such a decision right now.

This meditation ends the second phase of *The Spiritual Exercises of St. Ignatius.* In the first phase, *Challenge,* you focused on your life. In this phase, *Decision,* you focused on Jesus' teaching about life. The final phase, *Journey,* focuses on Jesus' death and resurrection and his invitation to journey with him into the unknown. Thus the decision you must make is this: Do you want to go on to the final phase, or do you want to take off a new months to decide?

This meditation also invites you to look to your future. Is there any decision concerning your future that the Holy Spirit seems to have led you to consider in the course of these "spiritual exercises"?

List some decisions you are now facing. *Speak to the Holy Spirit about each one.*

143

APPENDIX A

The Spiritual Exercises of St. Ignatius

The goal of *The Spiritual Exercises of St. Ignatius* is to help people find, choose, and live out God's will for them. The Exercises are divided into four parts, called "Weeks":

First Week—invites you to evaluate how well you are living your life according to the purpose for which God created you.

Second Week—shows how Jesus lived his life according to the purpose for which his Father sent him into the world and invites you to imitate and follow Jesus.

Third Week—strengthens and confirms your resolve to imitate and follow Jesus.

Fourth Week—begins your journey with Jesus to a fuller and richer Christian life.

The Exercises, or meditations, are normally made in a retreat house, where retreatants do them full time for thirty days. Saint Ignatius realized, however, that not everyone could take off thirty days to do this. So, in the 19th Annotation of his Exercises, he explains how the meditations can be done at home over a longer period of time. This meditation program is designed to help you do just that.

A popularized "text" of *The Spiritual Exercises of St. Ignatius* is *Modern Spiritual Exercises: A Contemporary Reading of the Spiritual Exercises of St. Ignatius* by David Fleming, available in Image (Doubleday) paperback.

APPENDIX B

Spiritual guide

The ideal spiritual guide for someone using this book is a spiritual director schooled in *The Spiritual Exercises of St. Ignatius*. If such a person is not available, a priest, minister, nun, brother, or lay person may serve as the spiritual guide.

The guide's role is to help the meditator come to grips with the meditation exercises in this book. The real work is between the meditator and the Holy Spirit. The guide is a kind of spiritual midwife in this important process.

A guide understands that you cannot really teach another person to pray. You can only share how you pray. A guide never forgets the words of Saint Therese of Lisieux:

One must banish one's own tastes and personal ideas and guide the other along the special way Jesus indicates for them, rather than along one's own particular way.

Finally, a guide is one who supports and encourages the meditator. This means being able to discuss the meditator's personal and home life, for these are bound to impact the meditator's ability to pray and come to grips with these exercises.

It goes without saying, therefore, that a guide must be secure enough to be rejected by the meditator and resilient enough to weather the difficult situations all spiritual guides encounter. Insecure people should not guide other people. Success is too important to them.

APPENDIX C

Small group meetings

The ideal group size is about eight to ten members, who meet weekly after completing each chapter. Begin each weekly meeting with the following prayer:

> *Lord Jesus, you said that*
> *wherever two or three gather in your name,*
> *you are there with them.*
> *We are two or three;*
> *we are gathered in your name;*
> *and we believe you are with us.*
>
> *May all our thoughts and sharing*
> *be guided by the Spirit and directed solely*
> *to the greater honor and glory*
> *of God, our loving Father.*

End each meeting with a Scripture reading (see suggested reading for each week). Allow a few minutes of silence following the reading. As the group solidifies in trust, the silence may be followed by a brief shared prayer. Conclude each meeting by having everyone join hands and pray aloud the Lord's Prayer.

A sharing guide for meetings follows. (One question is related to each meditation.)

WEEK 1　*Why do certain people excite you?*
Scripture reading: Psalm 33

1. What do you think gave Mother Teresa the courage to do what she did? What motivates others to follow her?
2. Who is someone you admire? Why that person?

3. What person (outside your family) has helped you as Jeff's friend helped him? Explain.
4. What do you admire most in your best friend?
5. Why do you think people are/aren't as open to challenges today as they once were?
6. What is the biggest challenge you have had to face so far in your life?
7. Why would/wouldn't you volunteer to serve with the leader described in this meditation?

WEEK 2 *How is Jesus different from other leaders?*
Scripture reading: Luke 5:1-11

1. What do you admire most about Jesus?
2. Why do you think Jesus does/doesn't impact human history as much as he once did?
3. What new lines has Jesus started you thinking along since you started meditating regularly?
4. Describe a time when you experienced Jesus' presence or power in your life.
5. What is one of your favorite gospel stories? Why this one?
6. Why do you agree/disagree with the statement that what the world needs *most* today is "not great minds, but great hearts"?
7. How are you answering Jesus' questions: "Is anyone out there? Does anyone care? Does anyone see what I see?"

WEEK 3 *Who is Jesus' mother?*
Scripture reading: John 2:1-12

1. What role does Mary, the mother of Jesus, play in your life?
2. What do you admire most about Jesus' mother?
3. If you were God and were looking for a mother to bear and rear Jesus, what are some traits you would be looking for? Why these?

4. When was the last time you turned to the mother of Jesus for inspiration or guidance?
5. Why do you think the role of Jesus' mother is given too much/too little stress today?
6. Why might some people like Franz Werfel and his wife experience what they did and still not become believers?
7. How can meditation on the mother of Jesus contribute to your understanding of Jesus?

WEEK 4 *Why did Jesus become one of us?*
Scripture reading: Luke 2:1-21

1. If Jesus were to be born today, where and under what circumstances might he choose to be born? Explain.
2. How does the incarnation teach us not only about God but also about ourselves? What is one of the biggest things it teaches us about ourselves?
3. What is the point of the parable of Mud Pie and Dry Leaf? How does it relate to Jesus?
4. Describe the last time you prayed to Jesus—really prayed.
5. What is the point of the parable of the watermelon hunter? How does it suggest why Jesus chose to live among us as he did?
6. Where do you experience Jesus' presence most convincingly today?
7. What "work of Christmas" could you begin doing in your life—right now?

WEEK 5 *Why did Jesus choose to live as he did?*
Scripture reading: Philippians 2:1-11

1. Why do/don't you think it is harder to follow Jesus during times of prosperity than during times of adversity?

2. How big a problem are loneliness and boredom in your life? If, as O.J. Simpson says, money and fame are not remedies for loneliness and boredom, what are?

3. If you asked your friends if you had too high or too low of an opinion of yourself, what might they say? Explain.

4. Describe a time when adversity revealed to you the true worth of a friend or family member.

5. Describe a time when something good you did went unrecognized and unrewarded. How did you feel about this at the time?

6. Distinguish between right pride and wrong pride. How do you keep the two separate?

7. How would you suggest a person try to cultivate a spirit of detachment from wealth, honor, and pride?

WEEK 6 *Are you free enough to follow Jesus?*
Scripture reading: Luke 14:15-20

1. What is the "pearl" in your life that you need to let go of if you want to follow Jesus more closely and live out God's plan for you?

2. Describe a time when you made a big sacrifice for another person, as Bill Havens did.

3. To what extent do you agree with this saying: "The only things we really keep in life are those we are willing to give away"?

4. Describe a failure in your life and how it helped you grow as a person.

5. In what part of your life do you feel that you are still only a "fan" of Jesus, and not yet a "follower"?

6. What is the point of the parable of the king and the young man?

7. What is one thing that threatens to keep you from being a Christian of the third class?

WEEK 7   *How much do you love God?*
Scripture reading: Luke 14:25-44

1. In what area of your life do you still tend to be a raft Christian?
2. Describe a time when, like Arthur Jones, you overcame peer pressure to do what you thought was right.
3. Describe a time when you supported someone who was under pressure, as Jackson Scholz supported Eric Liddell.
4. What is your biggest fear about trying to follow Jesus more closely than you now are?
5. Describe a time when you were pressured by others to do something you knew was wrong. From what sources do you seek to draw strength when you are under such pressure?
6. What was the most courageous thing you ever did? What motivated you to do it?
7. Describe a "conversion" experience in your life. In other words, describe a time when you "turned a corner" in your spiritual life, as Piri Thomas did.

WEEK 8   *Why was Jesus baptized and tempted?*
Scripture reading: Matthew 3:1-17

1. Since Jesus was without sin, why do you think he presented himself for baptism?
2. If Jesus set in motion God's kingdom on earth (the re-creation of our world), why is there still so much evil around?
3. How do you handle spiritual conflict when it occurs in your life?
4. Explain these two statements:
   a. "There's a silly idea about that good people don't know what temptation means."
   C. S. Lewis
   b. "Every evil to which we do not succumb is a benefactor."   Ralph Waldo Emerson

150

5. Why do you think Jesus allowed himself to be tempted by the devil?
6. What was a temptation that you recently experienced and overcame?
7. What facet of Jesus' life-style do you find most attractive?

WEEK 9 *How blessed are you?*
Scripture reading: Matthew 5:1-16

1. Recall a time when you experienced great joy in helping others, as Dr. Dooley did.
2. If your house were on fire and you could save only one thing, what would it be and why? What is the most valued item (apart from things like money, credit cards, and driver's license) that you carry in your wallet?
3. Describe an ugly situation that you handled (or saw someone else handle) in a lovely way, as the old couple did.
4. Describe a time when you showed mercy to another or were shown mercy by another.
5. Describe a time when you suffered "for the sake of Jesus."
6. How do you know what God is calling you to do?
7. Someone said, "Motivation is like a cable. As a cable is made up of many strands, so is our motivation." What are three motives (strands) that make up your motivation (cable)?

WEEK 10 *How ready are you to love as Jesus loved?*
Scripture reading: 1 Corinthians 13

1. How does the story "Metamorphosis" apply to your life in a very practical way?
2. Describe an incident from your childhood that made a deep impression on you.

3. Do you tend to love more than you are loved? Explain.
4. Describe a time when you passed up someone who was in need.
5. Why do you think Mother Teresa's order of nuns has grown rapidly at a time when most other religious orders have been declining?
6. On a scale of one (very easy) to ten (very hard), how difficult is it for you to show affection (hug or kiss) toward your father? Your mother? When was the last time you kissed one of your parents? What occasioned it?
7. How is the story of Don Quixote and Aldonza a story of Jesus and the human race?

WEEK 11   *How ready are you to forgive as Jesus forgave?*
Scripture reading: John 8:1-11

1. What makes it most hard for you to forgive others—your pride, your hurt, or what?
2. Have you ever prayed for the grace to forgive another or to be healed of a deep anger toward someone? If not, how do you handle these problems when they arise?
3. Explain Mr. Miyagi's warning to Daniel: "Who pursues revenge should dig two graves."
4. Why do/don't you agree that it is easier to forgive an enemy than to forgive a friend?
5. Why do you think Jesus commanded his disciples to "pray for those who mistreat you"?
6. What "key" to forgiving others is suggested by the story of the two soldiers?
7. Explain this statement: "People who can't or won't forgive break the bridge over which they themselves must travel if they are to reach heaven."

WEEK 12   *How ready are you to pray as Jesus prayed?*
Scripture reading: Luke 11:1-13

1. What time of day do you pray? Where do you pray? What posture do you usually take when you pray? How long do you usually pray?
2. Why are you inclined to agree/disagree that Jim Johnson's prayer brought about the transformation of his hotel?
3. Explain this statement: "Prayer is one of the ways that God shares his infinite power with us."
4. Describe a situation in which you prayed most fervently.
5. Why do so few people make use of the power of prayer that God has placed in their hands? Why don't you make better use of prayer?
6. Do you sometimes look up to heaven or speak out loud to God in your prayer? What prayers do you know by heart?
7. Explain these statements:
   a. "The act of praying is the highest energy of which the human mind is capable."
   Samuel Taylor Coleridge
   b. "Work as if all depended on you; pray as if all depended on God."   Saint Ignatius of Loyola

WEEK 13   *How ready are you to serve as Jesus served?*
Scripture reading: Matthew 20:20-28

1. What is the point of the story of the monk and his vision?
2. Describe some service project you got involved in to help people less fortunate than you.
3. Describe an occasion when you went out of your way to help someone who needed help.
4. Why don't more people live lives of service as Sister Emmanuelle does?

153

5. Describe a time when you shared your faith with someone.
6. Describe a time when you used your own money to help someone.
7. What need are you aware of in your home, school, parish, or community that you might be able to address creatively in some way?

WEEK 14 *How can you follow Jesus more closely?*
Scripture reading: Matthew 9:9-13

1. What was the most difficult decision you ever had to make?
2. Does taking "this world seriously" mean taking stands against evil, as Kim Chi Ha did?
3. How did you answer Schweitzer's question about indulging himself in pleasure while his brothers and sisters were enduring pain?
4. Do you ever think about the fact that God will someday demand an accounting of how well you used the talents he gave you? How are you trying to integrate this fact into your life?
5. Did saying DeLeo's prayer in a loud whisper assist you in praying it, or not? Explain.
6. How do you account for the difference in the way Pip treated the stranger the second time he met him, as opposed to the first time? What lesson might you draw from this?
7. Do you feel called to go on to the final phase of this meditation program?